CINCINNATI
MURDER & MAYHEM

ROY HEIZER

THE
History
PRESS

Published by The History Press
Charleston, SC
www.historypress.com

Front cover, top: courtesy of WCPO-9; *bottom*: courtesy of WCPO-9.
Back cover, top: topographical map of the city of Cincinnati, 1841, courtesy of the Library of Congress; *bottom*: photo by Roy Heizer.

First published 2021

Manufactured in the United States

ISBN 9781467148078

Library of Congress Control Number: 2021937209

Notice: The information in this book is true and complete to the best of our knowledge. It is offered without guarantee on the part of the author or The History Press. The author and The History Press disclaim all liability in connection with the use of this book.

This book is dedicated to all of the men and women
who were victims of these sinister stories.
May they all rest in peace.

CONTENTS

ACKNOWLEDGEMENTS

The author, Roy Heizer, would like to thank and acknowledge The History Press for the opportunity to tell the stories of Cincinnati's morbid and sinister history.

I would also like to thank my wife, Nancy, for all her help and support.

A special thank-you to my friend and fellow historian Tim Kraus. Without his help, the Coleman Avery story would not have been possible. I thank him also for permission to photograph items related to the story.

A profound thank-you to the *Cincinnati Enquirer*. Without its archives, this book would not have been possible. Cincinnati's longest-running newspaper has proved invaluable to my research, and it is greatly appreciated.

I would also like to thank the Ohio History Connection and the University of Cincinnati Library's online archives. Both have been extremely helpful for the research that went into this book.

I also thank all the business, church, synagogue, and community websites around Cincinnati for providing a wealth of information. You know your history better than anyone, and I thank you for sharing it with us all.

Appreciation goes to Dan Smith with Haunted Cincinnati Ghost Tour for spinning weird and wretched tales from the paranormal realm. I learned so much on your tour through Over-the-Rhine.

Last but never least, I would like to thank the citizens of Cincinnati, past and present. Together, they have created a rich and diverse history for all of us to study and understand. It is your stories I have tried faithfully to tell here. From the criminals who operated in the shadows, to the heroes who lead us through our bleakest hours, thank you one and all for what you have contributed to our amazing city!

INTRODUCTION

Cincinnati has always been a city of great diversity and extremes. In its 233 years, Cincinnati has seen the best and the worst of humanity and nature. Our local scientists have achieved noble goals, saving countless lives, while an influenza outbreak killed hundreds of citizens. German Americans created a legendary beer-brewing culture, while one of their own murdered them one after the other. We have built skyscrapers that were among the tallest in the world. At the same time, angry townsfolk destroyed an enormous courthouse during a time of unrest. Many Cincinnatians have become famous for their tenacity and accomplishments; others have become famous for their untimely deaths. A sunny day can turn into a fierce destructive storm in minutes. There are stories of shocking crimes that plumb the depths of human depravity, and tales of awe that send shock and blood across the headlines of yesteryear. The scales of justice oscillate, sometimes slowly, sometimes quickly, in "The City of Seven Hills."

Isaac Newton once said, "For every action, there is an equal and opposite reaction." That observation has never been more fitting than for Cincinnati.

Cincinnati Murder & Mayhem is a collection of stories from the sinister side of Cincinnati. The "Queen City," as locals call it, has always been a place of wonder and progress, but it has its darker side as well. These tales from the morose underside of Cincinnati create a backdrop of city life—and death—in the nineteenth and twentieth centuries. There are two sides to Cincinnati, so come explore mystifying stories of true crime, natural disasters, civil unrest, and more, all from the morbid side of greater Cincinnati's unrepentant history.

1
THE EASTER SUNDAY SLAUGHTER

Hamilton, Ohio, is a small town of sixty-three thousand residents about twenty miles north of Cincinnati proper. It's usually a quiet, safe, and friendly place in which to live. Large trees line neat streets, single-family homes, and the downtown features historic buildings, open parks, and the remnants of the Miami and Erie Canal. The local Christmas parade, trick or treating and Fourth of July celebrations bring the community together, while Thanksgiving and Easter bring families together. It has the feel of a small midwestern town, with the amenities of a larger city close at hand. To most folks, Hamilton must seem more Mayberry than Manhattan. It would be easy to forget the harshness of reality in Hamilton's bucolic nature, but sometimes, that perfect picture is shattered by a single headline.

On Easter Sunday, March 30, 1975, James Urban Ruppert murdered eleven family members in his mother's house at 635 Minor Avenue in Hamilton. The incident is now known as the Easter Sunday Slaughter.

Ruppert's early life was, according to court testimony, unstable. He was born on April 12, 1934. His mother, Charity, would tell him that she would have rather had a daughter. His father, Leonard, had a violent temper. He didn't care much about James or his brother Leonard Junior. As a child, James suffered from asthma and was not able to participate in a lot of activities due to the condition. James frequently told people that his mother hated him; he claimed that his mother beat him and encouraged Leonard to participate in the beatings.

The Ruppert family home. *Photo in public domain.*

Fortunately, or unfortunately for James, Leonard Sr. died in 1947, when James was twelve. Leonard Jr. became the father figure in the house and made life difficult for young James. Things got so bad that when he was sixteen, James tried to commit suicide by hanging himself with a sheet.

As an adult, James Ruppert was described as a quiet and helpful yet unremarkable man. The young man had no police record. James was jealous of his older brother's good job and family life. After two years, he flunked out of college while his brother earned a degree in electrical engineering and did well in athletics. Leonard Jr. also married James's ex-girlfriend, and the couple had eight children. Leonard had a good job with General Electric, while James was unemployed at the age of forty-one. James was a designer of jet engines and mechanical apparatuses by trade, but on becoming unemployed he moved back in with his sixty-five-year-old mother, Charity. The formerly semi-successful James had hit on hard times. He was described by those who knew him as a loner and an assiduous reader. His mother threatened to evict him because she was fed up with him not holding a job and his constant drinking. James also owed his mother and brother money. As pressure mounted on James, he withdrew into a world of solitude and alcohol.

A month before the massacre, James asked a gun store clerk about silencers for his weapons while purchasing ammunition. His behavior was becoming more unstable.

The night before the murders, like most other nights, James was out at the 19th Hole Cocktail Lounge, a bar where he talked with employee Wanda Bishop. She would later testify that James told her he was frustrated with his mother's nearly constant nagging and other family problems and that he needed to solve the problem. He left the bar at 11:00 p.m. but came back later. When Bishop asked him if he had solved the problem, he told her, "No, not yet." He stayed at the bar and continued drinking until it closed at 2:30 a.m. He then made his way home.

On Easter Sunday, March 30, 1975, Leonard Jr. was visiting his mother's house. He and his wife, Alma, brought their eight children to see their grandmother for the holiday.

James was upstairs sleeping off his previous night of drinking while the other family members enjoyed an Easter egg hunt in the front yard. Later, Charity Ruppert began cooking a meal while Leonard and Alma sat at the kitchen table. Most of the eight children were in the living room.

Around 4:00 p.m., James woke up, loaded a .357 Magnum, two .22-caliber handguns, and a rifle and went downstairs. He entered the kitchen and shot and killed Leonard Jr. first. The shot that killed Leonard was to the head. James then shot and killed his sister-in-law, Alma, and his mother, Charity, as she tried to stop him. Both received shots to the head. James left blood splattered all over the kitchen and three bodies sprawling in a pool of mingled blood. Next, he shot his nephew David in the head and his young and pretty nieces Teresa and Carol.

He then shot and murdered his niece Ann execution-style, as well as four nephews, Leonard, Michael, Thomas, and John. Why no one was able to escape or elude the gunfire would continue to be a mystery long after the smell of gunfire had dissipated. Busy with their own Easter celebrations, the shots, more than thirty, went unnoticed by neighbors.

For some unknown reason, James waited three hours in the blood-soaked house before calling the police to report the shooting. Patrolman Robert Minor was the first on the scene and found the bodies across two rooms. Three girls, a boy, and their father were found in the living room. The corpses of the two women and four of the children were found in the kitchen. All of them were riddled with bullets and soaked in blood. The police found James near the house, and he was arrested. The bodies, all eleven of them, were taken to Brown-Dawson Funeral Home in Hamilton. Questions arose immediately. How could eleven people be killed execution-style without any of them seeming to struggle or escaping? What turned an "ordinary" man into such a vicious killer? What happened during the three to four hours between the time of the shooting and when police were called? The whole case made no sense.

Dr. Garrett J. Boone, the Butler County coroner, said that all of the victims but one had been shot in the head. Police Chief George V. McNally said that four weapons, three pistols and a rifle, were found at the crime scene. All of the weapons had been fired. Police found thirty-one spent cartridges among the bodies. McNally described the suspect as "a gun freak," and it is believed that all of them belonged to James. When interviewed by police, a neighbor said that James did a lot of target shooting and knew how to handle a gun. All eleven members of the Ruppert family were buried in Arlington Memorial Gardens in Cincinnati.

For weeks after the shooting, the killing spree was all that neighbors in Hamilton and Fairfield could talk about. Many of them were asking the same questions as police. Why? How?

Reverend John Roettele described the Leonard Ruppert family as "a fine family" and active in their church. Neighbors, workmates, and schoolmates all described the large family as outgoing and gregarious. Leonard had no criminal record, and the police had never been called to their Fairfield home. The children, who attended Sacred Heart School, were well liked by their classmates and were good students. There was simply no indication that there was a troubled member of their family. Leonard never mentioned his brother's troubles to anyone. No one offered help, because no one knew that James was in a difficult situation—a classic case of appearances being deceiving.

The case went to the grand jury in early April. Ballistic evidence was sent to BCI (Ohio Bureau of Criminal Investigation) for examination. While Ruppert was in jail, his attorneys, Hugh Holbrock and Joseph Bressler, had him examined by both a psychologist and a psychiatrist. A sanity hearing was subsequently scheduled for May 12, 1975. Meanwhile, police continued to wonder why neighbors had heard no shots.

Ruppert pleaded innocent by reason of insanity. Professional psychiatrists and psychologists gave testimony during the sanity hearing, and Ruppert was found paranoid but able to stand trial. One psychiatrist testified that Ruppert was in "a paranoid psychotic state." One symptom, the psychiatrist testified, was "departure from reality in terms of thinking and behavior." The professionals also said that Ruppert had engaged in discussions with them that were normal and that he had the ability to recognize time and space. He spoke in a rational and organized manner. On the eve of the trial, set for June 16, 1975, Ruppert signed a jury waiver. He would be tried by a three-judge panel: Judge Fred B. Cramer, Judge Robert L. Marrs, and Judge Arthur J. Fiehrer.

The official trial started on June 16. In his opening statement, Butler County prosecutor John Holcomb stated that the murders had been motivated by money; that with his entire family gone, Mr. Ruppert would inherit $300,000, the family fortune. The prosecutor also called Ruppert's insanity defense a "scheme." He continued his opening statements by laying out the prosecution's case, laying the groundwork for the evidence that was to be presented. On opening day, fourteen witnesses gave testimony. On Monday, the three judges toured the home on Minor Avenue to get the layout of the crime scene. As the trial continued, evidence in the form of photographs, spent cartridges, clothing, and weapons were introduced into the court record. Dan Cappy, a blood expert, testified that three types of blood—A, B, and O—were found and that all three types were represented among family members. Fingerprint experts stated that prints lifted from the revolvers matched those of the defendant. The defense did not counter any of the evidence that the prosecution presented. Ruppert sat quietly in court as evidence was presented to the judges. Gaylord Morris Jr. and Donald A. Schwab both testified as to the financial holdings of Leonard Ruppert. The defense objected to several statements made by the prosecution, but to no avail. One witness, Ruby Lee, sister of Charity Ruppert and aunt of the defendant, testified that one of her sisters had been confined to a mental institution several years prior. She also testified that one cousin died in a psychiatric facility. She further testified that another cousin had committed suicide, and another had attempted suicide.

In his testimony, Dean Cavett, an employee of the gun shop that Ruppert frequented, stated that Ruppert had casually asked him about silencers. He testified that Ruppert wanted to know where he could get one. Vincent Isgro testified that he had seen Ruppert properly using a gun and thought Ruppert was "a superior shot to himself." This testimony was to establish that Ruppert was an adroit marksman who knew how to handle a handgun. The prosecution closed its case by reiterating their conclusion that the murders were financially motivated.

Counselors for the defense, Holbrock and Bressler, filed a motion for acquittal. The attorneys said that the prosecution had failed to establish prior consideration, a requirement for the charge of aggravated murder.

They also said the prosecution had failed to conclusively determine that James had any knowledge of his family's financial dealings. They argued that James would have had no idea what his mother's estate was valued at or what insurance policy his brother may have held. The judges quickly rejected the motion.

On June 21, 1975, the defense began to lay out their case. They testified in their opening statements that a question to Ruppert by his brother regarding Ruppert's automobile set Ruppert into a rage. Two defense professionals, Dr. Lester Grinspoon and Dr. Howard Sokolov stated that Ruppert was paranoid and could not control his actions. "In fact, if there had been more people in the house, they might have been killed also," Dr. Grinspoon testified in a grim tone of voice. Leonard frequently asked the question, "How's your Volkswagen?" in a condescending manner, setting James off. Grinspoon offered that this accumulated rage since childhood could be contained no longer. Years of hostility and tension exploded. Ruppert admitted to Dr. Grinspoon that he had shot his brother in the chest twice and then immediately turned the gun to the rest of his family. He then sat on the couch for two hours, contemplating suicide. However, he was Catholic and thought that suicide was a mortal sin, and he didn't want his last act to be a mortal sin. Grinspoon also testified that Ruppert was obsessed with the notion that his family and the cops were out to get him, and that this obsession was the most crucial thing in his life. He said Ruppert saw evidence of this conspiracy in everything: he thinks his cell is bugged and that his attorneys are in on it. Dr. Grinspoon diagnosed Ruppert as paranoid. Dr. Sokolov concurred with this diagnosis. They testified that after Ruppert shot his brother, his sister-in-law, and his mother, things became "hazy." James didn't remember much after that.

A Frisch's restaurant waitress, Valeta Sears, testified that Ruppert once told her he was "listening to Castro." The defense continued to stress Ruppert's mental condition. Through testimony, they stated that he could easily have gotten along in society without anyone suspecting his paranoid state of mind. Testimony was given that the condition was concealed in a veil of normalcy, rendering it virtually undetectable by an untrained person. A Cincinnati-based psychiatrist, Dr. Glenn Weaver, testified that he had treated Ruppert in the early 1960s, over ten years before the crime, but that Ruppert had ended the sessions abruptly. Dr. Weaver could offer no reason why Ruppert had suddenly ended their sessions. The defense called several additional witnesses, and they were cross-examined. These witnesses provided no new or compelling evidence that would change the trajectory of the trial. With the conclusion of witnesses, both the prosecution and the defense made their closing arguments before the three-judge panel. The prosecution continued to say that the crimes were financially motivated and that Ruppert knew what he was doing at the time. The defense's closing argument was that Ruppert was out of his right frame of mind at the time of the murders. They stated that he was driven by stress and a paranoid state. The defendant, according to court records, could not differentiate between right and wrong, moral and immoral, lawful and criminal.

The judges retired to make their decision.

The July 4, 1975 *Cincinnati Enquirer* headline read, "Judges Find Ruppert Guilty." Ruppert had been quickly found guilty of heinous crimes. The majority verdict also found that Ruppert was sane at the time of the murders. The only remaining issue was whether there were mitigating circumstances. In a separate hearing held after the initial trial, mitigating circumstances were established, ruling out the possibility of the death penalty.

On July 15, 1975, James Urban Ruppert was sentenced to eleven consecutive life terms, to be served at the Ohio State Penitentiary at Lucasville. During sentencing, Ruppert stood stone-faced, devoid of any recognizable emotion. He did not cry or even grimace. He simply stared through thick-rimmed glasses at the judges.

His lawyers appealed the verdict, but it was eventually denied. Parole was denied in 1995. Ruppert has been a model prisoner and has not caused anyone any problems. He spends most of his time sleeping or reading. Literature and unconsciousness remain Ruppert's two best friends. James U. Ruppert is eighty-six now and still serving his sentences at Franklin Medical Center in Columbus.

Eventually, the house of horror was cleaned up, and new owners moved in. They reportedly left after hearing odd voices and other unexplained noises that seemed to echo that fateful Easter day. However, the house has had other owners since. Due to its reputation in the neighborhood, it doesn't seem to hold a family for very long. Another family now occupies the infamous house. Please, don't bother the current owners.

2

PIATT PARK AND ITS SINISTER HISTORY

Piatt Park is the oldest city park in Cincinnati, dating to 1817. It was donated to the growing city by the Piatt brothers, Benjamin and John. It sits on a strip of land between Vine and Elm Streets. The park features statues commemorating two past presidents from Ohio. On the west end is a statue to William Henry Harrison; it is the only horse-mounted statue in the city. On the other end is a statue to James Garfield that was created by sculptor Charles Niehaus. Harrison and Garfield served the two shortest terms of any presidents. Harrison served 31 days, and Garfield served only 199. In addition to W.H. Harrison and Garfield, presidents who have hailed from Ohio include Ulysses S. Grant, Rutherford B. Hayes, Benjamin Harrison, William McKinley, William H. Taft, and Warren G. Harding. Although the official name is Piatt Park, some residents still refer to it as "Presidents Park" due to the statues at either end of the space. Over the years, the park has been the subject of several controversies and proposals. It has been suggested as a market, a parking lot, and a road. Several years ago, it was the location of an Occupy Wall Street encampment, an event that went on for several days.

Several high-profile crimes have occurred in Piatt Park over the years. In the 1970s, there was a string of unsolved pickpocket cases. In the early 2000s, an anarchy symbol was spray-painted on the base of the Garfield statue at the east end of the park. City officials did their best to remove it, but the granite is porous, and now, over ten years later, one can still see evidence of the graffiti. In 2014, Joshua Taylor, twenty-five, was shot and

The oldest park in Cincinnati, Piatt Park, has been the location of several strange occurrences. *Photo by Nancy Heizer.*

killed in Piatt Park. In 2019, a shooting incident involving a bicyclist and two men fighting happened in the park; the bicyclist was killed at the scene. In both shootings, a suspect was arrested. Despite its history, Piatt Park is a generally safe place to gather, and today it is a shady space to take a rest on a summer day.

Piatt Park is, however, not unique among the parks in Cincinnati. Every public space has seen at least one murder or strange death over the years. Not far from Piatt Park is Sedamsville Woods. It is known for the strange tale of "The Sleeper." According to property records, a farmer by the name of Sleeper occupied a farmhouse at the edge of the woods. Neighbors knew him as a bit of a hermit. He did not like folks coming on his land. The local kids, of course, had to test this, and more than a few of them were run off at the end of a rifle. If his rifle was not handy when local children or the wayward adult made their way onto his property, Sleeper was known to chase them off with the sharp blade of an axe. One time, he set his bull on an unsuspecting couple who thought they were just wandering through the woods. No one ever figured out exactly what his beef was. The folks guessed that he felt like he had a stake in seeing them gone.

Police records from 1956 indicate that Mr. Sleeper hanged himself in his barn on the property. It is a strange way for a man who liked his corner

Piatt Park has been the place for peaceful lunch dates, protests, and murder! *Photo by Nancy Heizer.*

of the world to go. There was an investigation, but his death was ruled suicide without explanation. The barn has long since been torn down, but the foundation still exists. If a hiker walks to the top of the hill now known as "Sleeper's Hill," they can still see the outline of the barn. Visitors swear there's a spot that can be made out that indicates exactly where Sleeper hanged himself all those years ago.

3
LAFCADIO HEARN AND THE TANYARD MURDER CASE

The *Cincinnati Enquirer*, Cincinnati's largest and longest-running newspaper, has been writing and publishing in the Queen City since 1866. The Cincinnati Enquirer Building was designed by Lockwood Greene & Company and completed in 1926. It was built of limestone and reached fourteen stories. In 1975, it was designated a historic landmark by the National Register of Historic Places (NRHP).

The *Cincinnati Enquirer*'s most notable writer is arguably Lafcadio Hearn. He was born Patrick Lafcadio Hearn in 1850. Though born in Greece, he spent most of his early years in Ireland. A strange and turbulent childhood was to unfold for Hearn. In his sixteenth year, his left eye was injured during an accident on a schoolyard. It became infected, and he would spend a year recuperating. He would remain blind in his left eye. Hearn also had myopia (nearsightedness), which left him with poor vision. For the rest of his life, he carried a magnifying glass and a pocket telescope at all times, believing that regular glasses would harm his vision even more. His condition explains why he always posed for photographs in profile, to hide his deformed left eye. At age nineteen, he was forced to immigrate to Cincinnati to live with relatives. The relative, a Mr. Thomas Cullinan, had little time or patience for the young Lafcadio. According to traditional knowledge, Cullinan gave Hearn five dollars, wished him luck, and put him out of the house. Hearn would later write of his experiences in 1869, being abandoned by relatives for a second time. "I was dropped moneyless on the pavement of an American city to begin life." Now homeless, Hearn began to frequent the local library.

Lafcadio Hearn, the *Cincinnati Enquirer*'s most notorious columnist. An eccentric man, Hearn detailed the Tanyard murder in horrific detail. *Courtesy of Holford Blog.*

He was sometimes thrown out of bookstores for perusing the shelves but never buying. Soon, though, he began to earn a little money reading for elderly folks and other groups. Despite having strange mannerisms and vision problems, Hearn was an excellent reader with an intoxicating vocal tonal quality.

Hearn had an affable personality, but he also had a dark side. While studying in France, he had become engrossed in gothic literature. The young Hearn was fascinated with and inspired by Edgar Allan Poe and followed in his footsteps by going into newspaper and literary work. Along with writing partner Henry Fanny, he became famous for his serial, *Ye Giglampz*, a satirical stab at art and society. His first published works in America, *YE Giglampz* appeared in the *Enquirer* in the early 1870s. In 1874, he began writing for the *Cincinnati Enquirer* full time, reporting on stories of crime and corruption. Hearn wrote about everything from tenement conditions to prostitutes who had been found hanging in their jail cells at the police station. He is infamous for his reporting in a series of articles and illustrations on the legendary Tanyard Murder Case, an 1874 Cincinnati murder.

It all started on November 7, 1874, on the day when *Harper's Weekly* ran a political cartoon by Robert Nast that was to be considered the first use of an elephant as a symbol of the Republican Party. It was also just a few days after the Democrats had won the U.S. House of Representatives for the first time since 1860. On that day, John Hollerbach heard screams emanating from the Freiberg Tannery on Livingston Street and Gamble Alley in Over-the-Rhine, a neighborhood of German immigrants. Hollerbach's window looked out on Gamble Alley, and the sixteen-year-old boy heard a fight break out near the tannery. He said he heard a man scream in German, "Für Gottes wille, Lass mich in Ruhe!" ("For God's will, leave me alone!").

Hollerbach got up and stumbled quickly out of the house to find a police officer. As he passed the tanyard, he heard a voice he recognized. It was Herman Schilling calling for the watchman and shrieking "murder!" The young man called out (in German), "Herman, is that you?" Schilling replied in a frantic tone of voice: "Yes, John, John, John. Come and help me; someone is killing me." Young Hollerbach then asked, "Who is it?," but the answer was unintelligible. Hollerbach shouted, "Murder, murder, let that man alone, or I will come in and shoot you!" He then left the scene and was unable to find a police officer and, becoming frightened for himself, returned home without making any outcry. On his way home, he thought he heard a dragging sound as if something was being pulled through the dirt streets. Strange noises such as banging and scraping could still be heard coming from the tannery, but the screaming had stopped. At long last, silence fell over the tanyard. The boy later told police that he kept vigilance the rest of the night and was frightened, but that he did not see Schilling or anyone else leave. Whoever it was, they had vanished in the night.

The next morning, one of the workers, Cornelius Westenbrook, arrived for his shift at the tanyard. He called out for Herman Schilling but got no response. Hollerbach heard him and ran over to tell his story, explaining with a raspy voice that he believed Herman Schilling was murdered there the night before. He said to Westenbrook, "I shouldn't wonder if Herman was killed last night." Westenbrook, alarmed, sent his son to get the police and to tell the owner of the tannery, Henry F. Freiberg, that an employee had most likely been murdered on company property. Westenbrook and Hollerbach then investigated, finding a gore-soaked scene, with blood sloshed on the barn walls.

Cincinnati police came in to investigate. Near the stable, they found signs of a fight. They also found two possible weapons: a sharpened wooden pole and a six-pronged pitchfork. Both items had fresh blood, and on one prong of the pitchfork, police discovered a small buckle like those used for braces (suspenders). Marks in the dirt indicated that a struggle had taken place.

Schilling lived on company property in a second-floor room that overlooked the tannery. He acted as sort of a night guard, to be there to look over things by night. Three large—and probably savage—mastiffs also guarded the grounds. Police searched his quarters, but they found no evidence of anything unusual. At that time, they had no idea what they were dealing with. They had no body and no evidence of a murder. If there had been a murder, they did not know where the corpse was taken. More blood was also found in the dirt, with a trail of blood leading to the boiler room, a distance of more than one hundred feet. The trail of blood wandered all the way to the door of the furnace. Someone suggested that the corpse may have been placed in the furnace to be eliminated. The business had a large furnace, and it was suggested that the heat it was able to generate could mimic a crematorium. Detectives agreed that the furnace was a good place to investigate.

Opening the furnace door, the police were quickly pushed back by the intense heat. However, one of the officers thought he noticed something suspicious in the flames. The fire was extinguished with cool water, and detectives extracted a charred human skull, a scorched human bone, and some nearly incinerated human flesh. The stench was of burning flesh, a putrid smell any good detective would have been familiar with. Among the smoldering ashes was a braces buckle that exactly matched the one found on the pitchfork prong. It did not take long for police to determine that the victim's body had been put into the raging hot furnace. Police had found their body. Had it been given a few more hours to burn, the evidence would have been lost. It was indeed murder.

Andrea Egner, a local businessman and saloon owner, and his son Frederick immediately became the prime suspects, on the evidence that the gate between the tannery and their property was wide open. They were arrested and charged with suspicion of murder and taken to the Olive Street Station, where they were booked. Samuel Bloom was put in charge of impaneling a jury, which consisted of John Cutter, George Gould, Henry Britt, John Wessel, B.F. Schott, and Dennis O'Keefe. They were required to view the charred and grotesque remains before the remains were moved to Habig's Undertaking Establishment on Sixth Street.

At the coroner's office, accompanied by Dr. P.F. Maley, *Cincinnati Enquirer* reporter Lafcadio Hearn drew a graphic and grotesque illustration of the charred remains. In the paper, he described the carnage this way:

> *The hideous mass of reeking cinders, despite all the efforts of the brutal murderers to hide their ghastly crime, remains sufficiently intact to bear*

frightful witness against them. On lifting the coffin-lid, a powerful and penetrating odor, strongly resembling the smell of burnt beef, yet heavier and fouler, filled the room and almost sickened the spectators. But the sight of the black remains was far more sickening. Laid upon the clean white lining of the coffin they rather resembled great shapeless lumps of half-burnt bituminous coal than aught else at the first hurried glance; only a closer investigation could enable a strong-stomached observer to detect their ghastly character—masses of crumbling human bones, strung together by half-burnt sinews, or glued one upon another by hideous adhesion of half-molten flesh, boiled brains, and jellied blood mingled with the coal.

Hearn further described the cranium:

The skull had burst like a shell in the fierce furnace heat, and the whole upper portion seemed as though it had been blown out by the steam from the boiling and bubbling brains!…The eyes were cooked to bubbly crisps in the blackened sockets, and the bones of the nose were gone leaving a hideous hole! On tearing away the frightful skull-mask of mingled flesh and coal and charred gristle, however, The Grinning Teeth showed ghastly white!

Hearn closely followed the developments in the case. He frequently accompanied the police on their rounds as they questioned witnesses and interrogated suspects. Hearn visited the coroner to get updates on evidence and procedure. It turned out that Andreas Egner and his son Frederick had been arrested for attacking Schilling with wooden rods in a prior altercation. The two had been convicted of assault and battery under Squire Benjamin C. True. Each had been fined $50 plus court costs. The two Egners were also put under a $200 bond to keep the peace for one year. Likely, they would have finished the job then had they not been interrupted by coworkers coming onto shift. The prime suspect owned a bar and a boardinghouse at 153 Findlay Street, directly west of the tannery. The gate between the tannery and Egner's bar was open the morning of Schilling's murder.

Herman Schilling, twenty-five, was an employee at the tannery. He had been rooming at Egner's boardinghouse until Andreas found him in a compromising position, in bed with Julia, Andreas' fifteen-year-old daughter. Schilling managed to escape through Julia's bedroom window. Egner must have thought that that was the end of it. However, when Julia turned out to be pregnant, Egner beat her and threw her out of the house for dishonoring the family name. She was thought to have lived on the streets for the next

Andreas Egner, the prime suspect in the Tanyard murder. He escaped the noose but did not escape justice. *Photo in public domain.*

few months. In her seventh month of pregnancy, Julia died, on August 6, 1874, under mysterious circumstances in the hospital. She was thought to have had cancer. Andreas Egner publicly accused Schilling of seducing his daughter, statutory rape, and subsequently being responsible for her death. The first attack on Schilling came on the day of Julia's death.

Schilling continued to claim that he was neither Julia's first, nor her lone, lover. He suggested that the father of Julia's baby could have been any number of men, and others in the neighborhood agreed. This is how Lafcadio Hearn described Julia Egner in a *Cincinnati Enquirer* article:

> *She was very fair, with that waxy mezzotint complexion almost peculiar to American-born German girls; very plump, bright, and playfully saucy, and possessing quite a graceful and womanly figure, although only between fifteen and sixteen years of age. Her father was never very kind to her, it seems, from what the neighbors say; and it is well known that he made use of her beauty to decoy customers into his saloon....Julia had many lovers, long before Herman was found in her bedroom. They used to climb in at night through the window of her bedroom on the west side of the building;*

*as many in that neighborhood have testified to the present writer and others.
The guilt of her seduction does not lie upon the memory of the unhappy
man who was so terribly sacrificed; and the father is not less to blame than
the real criminal.*

The police continued their investigation; eventually, a third suspect was arrested at his residence at 90 Logan Street. George Rufer had been fired from the tannery a few days before the murder and blamed Schilling for his redundancy. Blood was found on Rufer's clothes. "That is blood from the hides I handled," he told police. He could not give a sufficient reason why his face was covered in what looked like fingernail scratches and other scrapes, as if he'd been in a fierce fight. During police interrogation, Rufer testified that he was blocks from the tannery the night of the murder. He claimed that on the night that Freiberg laid him off, he went to Egner's establishment and had a few beers. After leaving, he went to a grocery store and had another beer and some wine. "I then went home to bed," he claimed. He further testified that he had on a previous occasion heard Andreas Egner say that Schiller should be run through with a pitchfork. Rufer also testified that the younger Egner had also publicly threatened the life of Schilling on several occasions. The evidence against Rufer looked circumstantial at best, but detectives kept him on the suspect list. By this time, large crowds had gathered at the tannery and at the Olive Street police station to glean any news they could of the ghoulish case. The group became so dense that it was described as "waves of the sea." It wasn't until a rainstorm opened up that the throng abated, to the relief of investigators.

Under long and strenuous interrogation from the police and coroner, all three of the suspects maintained their innocence. A hard man, Andreas Egner would not tell the police anything worthwhile. George Rufer told several contradictory stories but always tried to blame Egner. Rufer thought that he might come under suspicion if police tied his firing to the murder. He correctly felt that, in the eyes of the law, it would be a motive. Frederick Egner did not give any valuable information, but he also did not handle his interrogation well. He cried and whimpered throughout the questioning and during the proceeding night.

Hollerbach and Westenbrook both testified at the coroner's inquest to the events of Saturday night and to the conditions found at the murder scene that Sunday morning. They shared valuable and reliable information that was used at trial. George Rufer's wife testified that it had been her who had scratched George's face Saturday night in a scrap over money, but Rufer testified to the contrary, stating that he had gotten the scratches when he fell in the street. He later claimed that the marks on his face had come about when he jumped from a shed at Werk's factory. Frederick Egner testified that Rufer had been at the saloon Saturday night and gave testimony that implemented Rufer. The younger Egner said on the witness stand that Rufer stated boldly around the bar that he would "get Herman out of his job." Frederick testified under oath that he saw Rufer going toward the tanyard and heard Herman Schilling screaming, "Murder! Murder!" a short time later. (It turns out that it was Hollerbach who shouted those fateful words.)

In the presence of several reporters, including Lafcadio Hearn, Frederick Egner expounded on his testimony. He said that Rufer said of Schilling, "We will go over and kill that Low Dutch son of a bitch."

The investigation would reveal that Schilling was aware that Rufer had set a fire at M. Werk & Company's candle factory the prior Saturday; that Schilling was going to let the police know, thus giving Rufer a motive for killing Schilling. It was concluded that the assailants knew the premises and the layout well and were aware of the matter of the mastiff dogs to contend with. Likely, they brought meat with them to assuage the mastiffs. In testimony, Andreas Egner agreed. The plan was thus: The three men were to meet at 9:30 p.m. on Saturday night.

They hid in the tack room under the darkness of the night and waited for Schiller to come up from Gamble Alley. A tack room is where items related to keeping, training, and riding horses—saddles, harnesses, and horseshoes—are stored, and this would have made for the perfect hiding place. Schilling, unaware that he was being watched, went to the stable to tend to the horse. Rufer then came up behind Schilling and struck him with a piece of wood. Schilling fought back, but Rufer continued to beat him furiously with a stick. Andreas then plunged the pitchfork into Schilling's stomach. When Schiller began to scream, Rufer grabbed his throat and strangled him with his bare hands while Andreas continued stabbing him with the pitchfork. The whole attack took less than three minutes. Schilling lay still on the ground. No one, including the suspects, knew if Schilling was alive or dead at this point. He never, though, moved again on his own.

They discussed several ways to hide the corpse. At last, Rufer suggested burning it in the furnace. He tried in vain to get Schilling's body into the furnace, but it eventually took all three of them to get it through the small door. Rufer testified that they had to force it into the furnace.

A *Cincinnati Enquirer* article about the Tanyard murder. *Courtesy of Hamilton County Public Library.*

The three suspects made accusations and counteraccusations against one another. Egner called Rufer insane and so on. The next day, he repeated his confession on the witness stand. The inquest jury found that there was evidence to indict George Rufer and Andreas Egner for first-degree murder. The jury was also ready to indict Frederick Egner as an accessory. After the indictment, Rufer confessed but blamed the elder Egner for initiating the plot and for dealing the stab wounds that likely ended Herman Schilling's life.

During the inquest, as investigators dug deeper, more details about George Rufer came to light. As it turns out, he had a prior record and a secret. He had served prison time for horse theft. He also had another wife and child in Louisville and was, therefore, guilty of bigamy under Ohio law. Frederika, his wife in Cincinnati, had been deceived and was now left destitute. Records indicate that she sank into melancholy and lost her sanity. She tried to kill their eighteen-month-old daughter by slamming her head against a furniture chest. The child was sent to live with relatives, and Frederika would spend the remainder of her life in an institution.

At trial, the prosecution presented all the evidence they had collected during the investigation. They argued that Andreas Egner was the mastermind behind the plot and that George Rufer played a key role in helping him carry it out. The braces buckle, the pitchfork, and the charred skeletal remains were presented as evidence by the prosecuting attorneys. The first witness to offer any substantial evidence was Isadore Freiberg, son of the tannery proprietor. He testified that Schilling was a steady, hardworking man. He further testified that he knew about the animosity between Schilling and Andres Egner over his daughter and her relationship with Schilling and other men. As to Rufer's character, he testified that Schilling told him that Rufer was lazy and that he didn't like him, but he knew of no overtly ill feelings between Rufer and Schillings. Other testimony revealed that Rufer had publicly abused his wife on more than one occasion. The character of the Egners was also brought into question. It seems that they had had several scuffles that were generally known around the neighborhood.

The defense offered conflicting stories about where the suspects had been and when they had been there. They could offer no compelling evidence that would lead a jury to acquit them. They did not reach the threshold of reasonable doubt. During the trial, mobs gathered, and rumors circulated that they wanted to break into the station and lynch the suspects before the jury had its chance to deliberate. The suspects were moved to the reinforced and fireproof jail for their safety.

The jury heard the coroner's verdict. It was read aloud by Coroner Maley:

We, the undersigned Jurors, in Cincinnati Township and County of Hamilton, having been duly impaneled and sworn by P.F. Maley, Coroner, in and for the said county, to inquire and true presentment make, as to whom and by what means Herman Schilling, who's dead body was found at Freiberg's tanyard, corner of Livingston Street and Gamble alley, on the 8th day of November 1874, do hereby find the following verdict: "After having examined said body and heard the evidence, we the jury, do find that the deceased came to his death from violence inflicted by the hands of Andreas Egner and George Rufer. And we further find that Frederick Egner was an accessory to the fact; and to conceal the crime Andreas Egner, Frederick Egner, and George Rufer placed the body in the furnace at Freiberg's tannery, where it was partially consumed. And we are satisfied that the remains taken from the furnace are those of Herman Schilling, placed there by Andreas Egner, Fred Egner, and George Rufer on Saturday night, November 7, 1874.

Egner and Rufer were found guilty of murder and sentenced to death by hanging. However, one more twist was to befall Herman Schilling's justice. A writ of error was placed in the record and accepted by the Ohio Supreme Court. Egner and Rufus were to be given a new trial on a technicality; the prosecution had failed to adequately prove malice. When told he would receive a new trial, Egner sneered with a malicious look on his face. "I knew they wouldn't hang an innocent man," he said with a cynical tone to his voice.

Separate trials commenced for the two accused men, but the result was the same.

In the end, Andreas Egner was found guilty of murder and sentenced to life in prison. Rufer, who had not testified during the trial, eventually broke down and confessed his role in the murder but admitted much less than the evidence against him suggested. He claimed to be not much more than a witness when Maley and a reporter from the *Cincinnati Enquirer* questioned him after Andreas Egner's trial. Rufer was tried separately, and evidence both for and against him were brought forward. Many of the witnesses from the Egner trial were put on the stand. He, too, was found guilty of murder and sentenced to life in prison. In conclusion, only the sentence changed, but it did spare their lives.

Frederick Egner spent two years in jail on charges of accessory to murder while awaiting his trial. In the fall of 1876, Egner was set to go to trial. But the prosecutor was satisfied that no jury could be impaneled that could give him a fair trial. A change of venue would most likely result in an acquittal. Due to these circumstances, charges against him were eventually dropped.

George Rufer would spend the rest of his life behind bars. Andreas Egner contracted consumption in prison and was pardoned by the governor when it appeared that he was dying. He recuperated from the consumption and lived several more years. However, history notes that he died in 1889 as "a raging maniac."

Hearn wrote and illustrated an extensive serial on the Tanyard Murder Case for the *Cincinnati Enquirer*. His gruesome literary descriptions of the murder and illegal cremation were rivaled only by the shocking and graphic illustrations that accompanied the story. Due to his increasing notoriety, newspaper circulation went up dramatically, and Hearn was given a raise, from ten dollars a week to twenty-five dollars.

He went on to have a relationship with a mixed-race woman and was fired from the *Cincinnati Enquirer* and run out of town for it. He then went to the French West Indies on assignment. He spent the next ten years in New Orleans, writing about the city's culture before eventually settling in Japan. There, Hearn became even more famous for his books of Japanese folk tales and ghost stories.

The Cincinnati Enquirer Building, which is now a hotel, might be familiar to you as the home of radio station WKRP during the original run of the comedy show *WKRP in Cincinnati* as well as its sequel, *The New WKRP in Cincinnati*. On the show, the building was referred to as the Osgood R. Flimm Building.

4
COURTHOUSE RIOTS OF 1884

From the year that it was founded, Cincinnati has always been a city of extremes. In the early 1800s, it flourished and grew to be the sixth-largest city in America. But Cincinnati always had a dark underbelly. Social and economic tensions have been as much a part of the city as its buildings and innovations. Wealthy neighborhoods like Hyde Park were mirrored by areas such as Bucktown.

In the 1880s, Cincinnati was a rough-and-tumble industrial city with some of the most beautiful mansions in the Midwest. The city's population was exploding. German immigrants were pouring into the city. While prosperous Whites were moving up into the hills, the working class toiled in the basin. Regulations were almost nonexistent, and labor conditions suffered. Political corruption ran rampant, and the city was known for its high crime rate. Pork packing was one of the leading industries, and Cincinnati became known as "Porkopolis."

It was in the midst of these changing times that one of Porkopolis' most sensational crimes was committed. On Christmas Eve 1883, a young German man named William Berner and his accomplice, Joe Palmer, robbed and murdered their employer, William H. Kirk. A local businessman, Kirk owned a livery stable in the city's West End neighborhood. He was known to be a hardworking and honest man. Berner and Palmer's intention was to rob Kirk of $600. Kirk was hit over the head with a hammer from behind. They then beat him until he was nearly lifeless and then strangled him with a rope until he died. The two murderers then dumped Kirk's body in a culvert of Mill Creek, just upstream from the Miami and Erie Canal, near the community of Cumminsville (later renamed Northside). It would be three days before the crime was discovered. After the body was found by Adam Fisher, an investigation ensued. This investigation found that, among other things, Kirk's horses had not been fed or watered for three days. This helped establish a timeline. The exact amount stolen was never realized.

Berner and Palmer were soon named prime suspects and arrested. A trial date was set. The *Cincinnati Enquirer* noted that five hundred potential jurymen were called before Berner's lawyer, T.C. Campbell, accepted twelve men to be jurors. Thomas C. Campbell was the leading criminal defense attorney in Cincinnati and head of the local Republican political organization.

After a prolonged trial, on March 26, 1884, the jury returned a verdict of manslaughter, not murder, as the public wanted—this despite the witness testimony by seven people who said that Berner had admitted his premeditation and guilt of the murder. In Ohio, in 1884, the law stated that no one could be executed for manslaughter, as it was not a capital offense. The judge called the verdict "a damned outrage" and sentenced Berner to the maximum, twenty years at the state penitentiary.

The next day, the *Cincinnati Enquirer* and the *Cincinnati Post* called for a public meeting to denounce the verdict. Long pent-up anger at a less than effective legal system was about to meet its breaking point. Little did the newspapers realize the fuse that they lit. The jury, the judge, and some newspaper reporters failed to realize the barely contained outrage the public had for what they perceived as injustices. They were tired of criminals being let go or treated lightly while elected officials indulged in all manner of corruption. They were tired of trying desperately to make a living wage while criminals escaped justice.

Palmer, a mixed-race man, was put in a separate jail cell. He attempted to deny his identity, claiming he was not Palmer. He even tried to claim that he was a White man. Eventually, though, he broke down and confessed his identity. He also confessed to his part in the murder and robbery, stating that Berner did the actual killing and robbing and that he just helped with logistics. T.C. Campbell made sure that Palmer was tried separately. He was quickly convicted and hanged.

The unorganized meeting with unclear purpose turned out to be a catalyst for the deadliest riot in Cincinnati history. We have had several bloody and destructive riots. General Andrew Hickenlooper,* Dr. Andrew Kemper and Judge Carter all spoke to the crowd of about ten thousand

---

*Author's note: General Andrew Hickenlooper is an ancestor of mine.

people. Their rhetoric may have incited the crowd even further. Chants of "Hang him" could be heard. A noose was thrown at the speakers. The crowd, wanting justice, began to erupt on Wednesday, March 26, 1884. At first, it was just a few dozen folks chanting in the streets. But soon the mob began to get more aggressive.

It was reported that one of the jurors, James Bourne, had to spend the night at the Bremen Street police station after being threatened by the unruly citizens. Bourne returned home on the morning of March 27, 1884. However, a crowd was waiting for him and threatened to lynch him. Luckily for Bourne, the crowd was dispersed by the Cincinnati police. Later, he was severely beaten by the angry mob and was again taken into custody at the jail infirmary for his safety. Charles Dollahan, another member of the jury, had rotten eggs thrown at him. He did not return home. Shots could be heard randomly throughout downtown. Windows were smashed. A man by the name of Louis Havemeyer, who had been on the jury, was told he was fired from his place of employment. The crowds were growing bigger and more aggressive. A crowd ripped the blinds from the house of a man named Phillips. The unruly mob threw dead cats and rotten vegetables through the windows before realizing they had the wrong house. That Phillips was not a member of the jury. The judge was put under police protection. Several small fires were set when the jail was ransacked. The jury foreman, A.F. Shaw, went into hiding for his life.

The next day, Friday, March 28, 1884, saw even more civil unrest. Colonel C.B. Hunt, commander of the Ohio Militia, came to Cincinnati with four hundred men. They prepared for trouble. They set up guard half a block from the courthouse. That evening, several thousand protesters headed to the jail, apparently planning to lynch Berner. Unknown to the rioters, Berner was not there. He had already been sent to the Ohio State Penitentiary in Columbus for his safety. He escaped when a mob attacked him while being transported in a coach through Loveland. The next morning, he was captured in Morrowtown. He was taken to the penitentiary to serve his sentence.

Hamilton County sheriff Morton Hawkins was ready for rioters. He had thirteen deputies and some volunteers helping him watch the jail. The rioters somehow managed to break into the jail through Hawkins' private quarters. However, they left when they were shown that Berner was not there. More rioters then arrived. Hawkins rang the riot alarms, which had the unintended consequence of drawing out more citizen rioters into the mayhem.

The mob barraged the jail with bricks, debris and stones. They overwhelmed the guards and police reinforcements. They retook the jail. They were driven out by reinforcements from the militia armory that entered the building through a tunnel from the courthouse. One of the attackers was shot and killed by the militia, and the violence escalated from there. Rioters attempted to set the jail on fire using stolen kerosene. By the time the situation became temporarily under control late on Friday night, five people had died, including one police officer. Several dozen rioters were injured, as well as several citizens who were not participating.

On Saturday, March 29, Cincinnati woke to an *Enquirer* headline: "At Last the People Are Aroused and Take the Law into Their Own Hands, Enraged Community Rises in Its Might." The city leaders, who had at first supported the rioters' actions, became alarmed. They began to wonder if the mob was led by socialists and anarchists. They labeled them the "dangerous classes." Rioting continued sporadically throughout the day. Later on, Saturday, the governor of Ohio, George Hoadly, was asked to call in National Guard reinforcements. He did not order additional deployment units until the evening of March 29.

The entire reaction was a mess from the start. A number of the guards failed to report for duty at all. Some were undertrained and did not know how to handle large, unruly crowds. Some of the First Regiment soldiers even participated in the riot. The nonlocal soldiers, many of whom did obey the orders they were given, were unable to reach Cincinnati in time to prevent the escalating violence. Rioters who had been paid that day went out to the beer houses in Over-the-Rhine and got drunk. The intoxicated citizens added even more volatility to the situation.

During the day, the defenders of the jail erected barriers in the surrounding streets improvised from household goods, construction materials, grindstones, railing, and barrels. The militia was forced to abandon the armory and move to the jail with all the arms and ammunition. The jail infrastructure was about to collapse. Extremely crowded and ill-equipped to feed the prisoners, the jail was overrun. Policemen numbering 200 to 300 were present, although they refused to play an active role in the defense of the city. In addition, 117 local militiamen and the criminal occupants of the jail were involved.

In the evening, the mob gathered again in front of the courthouse and the jail. A gunfight broke out, lasting several hours. A group of Ohio militiamen tried in vain to guard the courthouse. The fighting over access to the courthouse cost several people their lives, including John J. Desmond. A local lawyer and captain of the militia, Desmond was shot and killed by an unknown rioter during the siege on the courthouse. The crowd managed to set fire to the courthouse and blocked attempts by firemen to put out the blaze. In the days of paperwork, paper records and no building fire codes, there was plenty inside the building to set on fire. The courthouse was destroyed. Hundreds of thousands of records were destroyed. File cabinet after file cabinet burned to ashes. Valuable documents, including historical records, were lost.

Rioters also started breaking into nearby stores. One store owner and his assistants shot three looters dead.

Eventually, reinforcements started to arrive by train. A force of three hundred militiamen from Dayton joined the melee three blocks from the courthouse, but then, at the sight of the confusion, retreated to the railway station. Another group of more resilient militiamen from Columbus arrived at around 11:00 p.m. They were armed with a Gatling gun and managed to clear the streets around the jail and courthouse. However, fighting continued elsewhere in the city until 3:00 a.m.

On Sunday, March 30, the *Cincinnati Enquirer* changed its storyline. In its Sunday-morning edition, it described the ongoing rioting as "Fire and Fury, the Reign of Terror" and "Awful Scenes in Cincinnati." Despite a growing number of militiamen and police, the riots resumed on Sunday. There was one more round of violence on the militia before calm returned to the city. Smoke rose from several locales around Cincinnati as an eerie calm gripped the city. The riots, for reasons unknown, had worn themselves out.

Though Cincinnati was for the moment quiet, Secretary of War Robert Lincoln had called in U.S. troops. When they arrived the next day, there was little for them to do. They remained on call for the next week in case of further rioting. The rioters had returned home, and calm had at last been restored. Over the course of four days, the riots had devastated the city. The fighting took the lives of fifty-six citizens and left more than three hundred wounded. Property loss was in the millions. The loss of court records was incalculable, with ramifications lasting for decades.

In the days after the outburst, newspapers fell on both sides of the issue. The public reaction in some publications was sympathetic to the rioters; others were not. The *Commercial Gazette* published an editorial saying: "The time has come for taking an account for salvage for three days of destruction and terror. First, we have saved our jail full of murderers. We have killed forty-five innocent men and wounded or maimed forty-five more, all to save a jail full of murderers." The editorial went on to describe the riots as "just, popular impulse against the prostration of laws before criminals." On March 31, 1884, a report in the *New York Times* said there was a feeling that the militias were responsible for most of the deaths. Their presence had incited the mob into outrage, and they had been all too ready to shoot on the crowds.

Harper's Weekly blamed intelligent citizens who had conceded people's politics to corrupt politicians. The magazine called for new laws with "swift, sure, and solemn" execution. It stated that if average citizens were running the government instead of corrupt special interests, incidents like the Courthouse Riot would never have occurred in the first place.

The riots ended the reigns of political bosses John R. McClean and T.C. Campbell. McClean ceased practicing law and returned to private life. Campbell faced disbarment proceedings. William Howard Taft would serve as one of the prosecutors, but they would fail to have Campbell ousted.

Although Berner was initially given a twenty-year sentence, he was granted parole after serving a mere eleven years. He had been seventeen-years-old at his conviction and, at his release, was a man of less than thirty. The *Cincinnati Enquirer* described him as "a tall handsome young man, who's stripped clothes and convict's cap ill-concealed his intelligent countenance and his dignity of bearing. The decade and more had wrought a complete change. Indeed, it might be called a transformation."

After he had served his sentence, Berner came back to Cincinnati to visit City Hall. He first looked up Watchman Tom Howells, who had been his guard at the penitentiary. Berner then requested to see Mayor Caldwell, and the request was granted. He announced that he intended to return to Columbus but wanted to see the mayor before he left. From the mayor's office, Berner was shown around City Hall. He was brought to the police area, where he met several policemen who remembered him. On meeting Berner, Chief of Detectives Hazen bluntly told him he should have been hanged along with Palmer. The brash statement upset Berner, and it was reported in the *Enquirer* that "in whose [Berner's] eyes could be noticed tears as he walked out of the office." After leaving City Hall, Berner went to Third and Walnut to see ex-banker E.L. Harper, a man he had known in prison. Berner was registered at the Emery Hotel, the same locale where T.C. Campbell, who had been his lawyer during the trial, was also registered. Campbell and Berner spoke briefly, a conversation in which Campbell stated his support for Berner's release. Berner, according to the *Enquirer*, told Campbell that he had a job in Columbus working for a fruit dealer. He also stated his intention to lead a normal, honest life. After the encounter, Campbell left Cincinnati to work in New York.

The courthouse was soon rebuilt on the same location. However, in 1914, it was torn down. The current edifice was erected in 1915. The current Hamilton County Courthouse, constructed in the Greek revival style, was built with several fire and riot safety features in mind. It is almost completely made of stone, marble, and metal—materials that cannot burn. Reinforced doors and windows were added to prevent rioters from being able to enter.

A statue of John J. Desmond, the lawyer and captain of the Ohio Militia who was shot dead while trying to protect the courthouse, stands in the lobby of the current courthouse.

5
AVONDALE RIOTS OF 1967 AND 1968

The 1960s was a tense time in America. The assassination of President John Kennedy and the civil rights movement caused political tension. The Vietnam War and its effects on the culture at large made headlines day after day. The counterculture and the Black Panthers rattled traditional institutions. Unemployment and protests ran rampant across America. It was no different in Cincinnati. Stress and anxiety were at an all-time high here as well. Cincinnati has always been a diverse city, with heavy populations of minorities; racial tensions have been a long-standing part of the city's culture.

In May 1967, Posteal Laskey Jr., a letter carrier who had chosen his victims based on his mail route, was convicted as the "Cincinnati Strangler." Laskey was a Black man who had been accused of raping and murdering six White women. He was Cincinnati's first Black serial killer. During his trial, Laskey's cousin Peter Frakes picketed outside the courthouse with a sign that read, "Cincinnati Guilty—Laskey Innocent!" His protest led to a small gathering of angry citizens who thought the police were targeting the Black community.

Frakes was arrested for blocking the sidewalk. Enraged Black leaders held a protest of his arrest on June 12, 1967, in the Avondale neighborhood, at the Lincoln statue on the corner of Reading and Rockdale Roads. At some point, the protest got out of hand. The rioting began on June 12 and lasted for several long days and nights. A thousand rioters came out in force to smash windows, fences, and mailboxes. Protesters carried signs

Huge plumes of smoke can be seen rising over Avondale as fires burned out of control in 1967. *Courtesy of the* Cincinnati Enquirer.

that demanded equal justice. They looted stores of cash and merchandise. They attacked cars, breaking doors and puncturing tires. Buildings and apartments were not spared. Fires were set, and graffiti marred walls. While most protesters just wanted to peacefully have their voices heard, some folks came out to cause trouble. The *Cincinnati Enquirer* sent in reporters to witness the disturbance and report to the newspaper. Local television reporters had rocks thrown at them. One witness to the outrage reported, "There's not a window left on Reading Road or Burnett Avenue. The youths are doing it and adults are standing by and laughing." A reporter made the comment that "While most of the rioters were legitimately angry and justified in their outburst, some of those participating were just out for themselves; taking advantage of the situation to steal something under the cover of the chaos." People marched in the streets shouting slogans and spiting at cops.

The rioting spread from Avondale to Walnut Hills, Bond Hill, Corryville, Clifton, the West End, and downtown. The *Cincinnati Post* reported that a fifteen-year-old boy was critically wounded in front of a fire station when it was being fired upon by a car full of rioters. The Cincinnati Fire Department was called to Avondale multiple times over the twelve days of rioting. According to an Avondale resident, rioters were protesting constant harassment by the Cincinnati police, as well as high unemployment, general dissatisfaction with city leaders and store owners "jacking up prices and selling bad products." Many small store owners boarded up their businesses.

After almost two weeks of violence and vandalism and no end in sight, Governor James A. Rhodes ordered seven hundred Ohio National Guardsmen into Cincinnati to quell the rioting. The National Guard was put on patrol in the streets in army-green jeeps. They were armed with machine guns and were ordered to kill if they were fired upon. They patrolled the streets as if Avondale was under martial law. Their presence intimidated locals who were just trying to go about a normal routine and further agitated the rioters. Luckily, the rioters avoided the Ohio National Guardsmen, and no rioters were shot. The rioting lasted until June 15, 1967. In total, the riot cost one person their life. It left sixty-three people injured. Over four hundred residents had been arrested, Dozens were left homeless, and Avondale had endured more than $2 million in property damage.

Less than a year later, riots erupted in the neighborhood once again. The 1968 riots were a reaction to the assassination of Martin Luther King Jr. on April 4. Tension in Avondale had already been high due to a lack of job opportunities for Blacks. The assassination of the civil rights leader only escalated that tension. On April 8, around fifteen hundred Blacks attended a peaceful memorial held at a recreation center in Avondale. A beautiful spring day was about to turn into a nightmare.

A high-ranking officer of the Congress of Racial Equality blamed White Americans for King's death and spurred the crowd to take action and retaliate. However, the crowd was orderly when it left the memorial and spilled out into the street.

As the crowd was leaving the memorial, James Smith, a Black man, was attempting, with his own shotgun, to protect his jewelry store from a robbery attempt. During the struggle with the robbers, who were also Black, the shotgun went off and Smith accidentally shot and killed his wife. A false rumor was spread in the crowd that Smith's wife was killed by a White police officer, and the rioting started soon thereafter. What started as a simple protest quickly escalated into a full-scale riot. Dozens of rioters smashed store windows up and down Reading Road and looted stores' merchandise. More than seventy fires were set across the neighborhood, and several of them turned into major outbreaks. Molotov cocktails were thrown, starting even more fires. During the rioting in Mount Auburn, a large group of rioters dragged a young man and his wife from their car. Noel Wright was stabbed to death in the street, and his wife was beaten unconscious. Noel Wright's killer was obviously there to cause trouble, not to protest injustice. His murderer was never identified or apprehended.

They simply disappeared back into the crowd. Protesters were upset that the cops arrested peaceful folks while not pursuing justice.

The next night, by order of the mayor, the city was put under curfew. Most residents obeyed the curfew, but many did not. Those who were out to cause trouble continued rioting long into the night. Nearly fifteen hundred Ohio National Guardsmen were once again brought in to subdue the unrest. Several days later, two people were dead, hundreds were under arrest and Avondale and its surrounding neighborhoods had suffered more than $3 million in property damage. This was twice the damage of the prior year's rioting. Avondale's flourishing business district along Burnet Avenue had been destroyed by the riots of 1967 and 1968. What had been a quiet, quaint area now looked like a war zone.

Many of the affected areas were left vacant for decades. Some of the side streets have never recovered. Several churches and two synagogues moved out of the neighborhood, abandoning historic buildings that had, in some cases, stood for a century or more. The riots helped further the image that the city was too unstable and dangerous for families. This perception, right or wrong, helped fuel "White flight" to the farther-out suburbs. Families,

Cincinnati cops patrolling during the Avondale riots. *Courtesy of the University of Cincinnati.*

both Black and White, that were better off financially and educationally left areas like Avondale. Those people who remained found they had less opportunity for success and that the image of the neighborhood had suffered. Neighborhood stores that had served the community were closed. With those closures came unemployment. What had been a prosperous and safe place to live was now destitute and struggling with self-sufficiency. A more bureaucratic effect of the riots was that insurance companies ceased to cover new businesses in Avondale. It was considered a high-risk area and not economically feasible to cover businesses that might just get looted again. Without the ability to obtain insurance, many businesses were doomed to fail before they even got started. The Fair Housing Act of 1968 was supposed to end what was called "redlining" in the real estate industry, but insurance companies saw to it that the act was stifled.

To the east of Avondale were the wealthy and White neighborhoods of Hyde Park and Oakley. These areas were left untouched by the rioting, as were Clifton and Corryville to the west. The latter two neighborhoods were protected due to their proximity to the University of Cincinnati and the Hebrew Union College as well as medical centers. It is no coincidence that they were almost entirely White. To Cincinnati's White population, Avondale was just an unpleasant neighborhood that connected more upscale environs.

In the 1960s, the city of Cincinnati lost 10 percent of its population, compared to a loss of just 0.3 percent in the 1950s. Cincinnati would continue to lose residents every decade afterward. Avondale and many of

The 1967 riots in Avondale. *Photo in public domain.*

the neighborhoods around it experienced steep urban decline in the years after the riots. It may take decades for many neighborhoods to recover financially from the riots.

The destructive nature of the riots led to negative consequences for Cincinnati's Black neighborhoods. In 1967, all of Cincinnati's city council members were White (although Theodore M. Berry had been elected to the city council in 1949). Several city boards were also all White. However, after the riots, a representative number of Blacks were appointed to city boards and commissions. Soon afterward, Blacks were elected to the city council. It was not until 1972 that Cincinnati elected Theodore M. Berry as its first Black mayor. Avondale may have been decimated during the riots of 1967 and 1968, but it never lost being called a neighborhood. Today, it still shows the scars of those riots. Large parts of the neighborhood are still boarded up. However, there are encouraging signs that Avondale is slowly beginning to make a comeback.

6
THE STRANGEST ROOM IN THE HOUSE

Cincinnati thrived during the Victorian era, and prosperous businessmen like Jacob Schmidlapp and Henry Probasco attained wealth and status. Cincinnati was one of the largest cities in America, and it had large numbers of Victorian homes to show for it. Grand mansions built by famous architects such as Samuel Hannaford and William Tinsley can be found in neighborhoods like Clifton and Hyde Park. While these homes vary in their look and feel, they all feature a parlor room at the front of the house. The parlor was a formal room, not for everyday use. It was kept in immaculate condition and featured the family's best furniture. Large area rugs and fancy drapes accented the importance of the room. The parlor was most often used for receiving guests, but occasionally it was used for a more somber purpose.

During the Victorian era, people were much more likely to die in their homes than in a hospital or a rest home. Doctors made house calls, and hospital admissions were reserved for the worse cases. Families were larger, medical practices were more rudimentary and death was a common part of everyday existence. Almost every family, even the wealthy ones, knew death all too well. The reaper came calling for the young and old alike. There was also no place beyond the city morgue to take and care for the deceased.

While the actual funeral was held at a church or a synagogue, the parlor became the main space in which the visitation or wake was held. Often, the casket was on display in the parlor for those in mourning to gather and grieve together. If a mortem photo of a child or adult was going to

A typical Victorian-era parlor, a formal room at the front of the house where guests were received. *Courtesy of wordpress.com.*

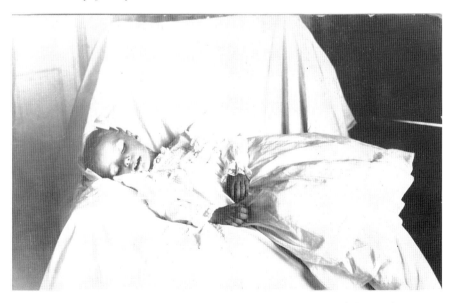

A Victorian-era mortem photo from the late 1800s. A mortem photo might have been a person's only portrait. *Courtesy of William Clements Library.*

be taken, it was generally taken in the parlor. A mortem photo is the last portrait taken of someone after death as a keepsake for the family. In an era before photography was common, a mortem photo may have been a family member's only photo. As creepy as it may seem to us today, it was a common practice in the Victorian era.

By the first decade of the twentieth century, Cincinnati had several funeral parlors. A funeral parlor was a business down the street where the deceased and their families were taken care of, a place that was nicely decorated where families could gather to view the dead. If a mortem photo was going to be taken, it was now taken at the funeral parlor. The Victorian era was drawing to a close by 1902, and times and traditions were changing. Mortem photos were no longer "en vogue"; the practice seems to have died along with Queen Victoria.

The parlor was no longer used for wakes and visitations, and it garnered new life. It transitioned to a room where happy families could gather for games or lively conversation on the topics of the day. The parlor also took on a new name. No longer used as a death room, it became known as the living room.

THE RHINOCK REPORT

When Joseph L. Rhinock was elected to the U.S. House of Representatives from Covington, Kentucky, in the November 1904 elections, he came with an impressive list of accomplishments. He had been president of the Covington Public Library Board for two terms. He had served on the Covington City Council. Rhinock had also served as mayor of Covington from 1893 to 1900. He would serve Kentucky in the House from 1905 until 1911. The Robert W. Criswell scandal marred Rhinock's time in the U.S. House of Representatives. During his tenure, Rhinock sued Criswell, the editor of the *New York Times*, for libel.

Criswell had started in publishing work by drawing illustrations for the *Cincinnati Commercial* publication. For a year, he wrote articles for the *Cincinnati Enquirer* about the Indiana legislature. He was later on the regular staff as a writer for the *Enquirer*. By 1905, Criswell had moved to the *New Yorker*, a weekly publication. Throughout his career, Criswell had been a humorist, publishing funny sketches and stories on the topic of the day.

On June 21, 1905, Criswell published an article titled "An Insult to Alice Roosevelt," which insinuated that President Roosevelt's daughter Alice was being used by Ohio congressman Nicholas Longworth to position himself for the advancement of his career. It also indicated that Longworth introduced Alice to several questionable characters, including racetrack bookies who indulged in all kinds of criminal activity, including murder, and Kentucky representative Joseph L. Rhinock, a politician who had reportedly been indicted for stealing fifty dollars. When Rhinock read the article, he was outraged that his character had been attacked.

Portrait of Robert W. Criswell, the man at the heart of the Rhinock Report. *Photo in public domain.*

Rhinock filed a criminal libel suit against Criswell and the *New Yorker*. Criswell was arrested on a charge of slander. When he spoke to investigators, he claimed that a Cincinnati-based correspondent whom he trusted wrote the article. The reporter had read Rhinock's indictment report. Criswell hired an attorney and was released on $1,000 bail. With the public and a popular newspaper on Criswell's side, a trial was set for September. However, Criswell confided in friends that he was nervous about the upcoming proceedings. He put on a confident public face, but in private, he was upset by the charges. Usually a man of humor, Criswell grew more and more morose.

Before the trial, on August 3, 1905, Criswell, who was "evidently under stress of great excitement," as one witness was quoted as saying, charged down the steps of the Seventy-Second Street subway station, darted at frantic speed beside a moving train, jumped in front of the cars, placed his head and hands on the rail and was killed instantly as the train ran over him. Witnesses said that blood, bone, and skull fragments were left smeared all over the tracks. Both hands had been ripped off, and he had been almost completely decapitated. What remained of him was dragged down the tracks for several yards, splattering blood as it went. One witness swore they saw moving fingers on the smog-covered gravel beside the tracks after the train had passed. It took the coroner's office several hours to get the gruesome scene cleaned up.

After his death, it was revealed that Criswell and *New Yorker* publisher Robert A. Irving were suspected of perpetrating a fraud. They were thought to be fleecing their subscribers. Paul Krotel, assistant district attorney for New York, made a statement regarding the investigation: Criswell and Irving collected $6,500 from subscribers for a book that would be named *America's Foremost Families*. However, on reviewing the project's accounting, no funds had been spent on materials (pens, ink, paper, etc.). There was no evidence that any part of the book had been written. Investigators failed to uncover so much as an outline. Krotel said Criswell "was very nervous and scared the last time he was here, and I am not greatly surprised to hear of his death."

The coroner officially declared Criswell's death a suicide after two witnesses testified under oath that Criswell threw himself in front of the approaching train. No other suspects were questioned in the incident, and the case was officially closed. History notes that Criswell's body was taken to Aurora, Indiana, on the outskirts of Cincinnati for burial.

After Criswell's death, Irving was jailed in connection with the libel suit and on fraud charges. The libel suit resumed in October. Results of that suit remain unlocated, but it is known that Irving died of heart disease in

Left: The mausoleum of Joseph Lafayette Rhinock, a congressman, a mayor, and a shadow on the light of decency. *Photo by Nancy Heizer*.

Below: The crypt of Joseph L. Rhinock. *Photo by Nancy Heizer*.

his New York home at the age of fifty-nine. The *New Yorker* was defunct by January 1906. The entire case is still somewhat of a mystery to historians. It may never be known if Criswell committed suicide from guilt over the slander against Alice Roosevelt and Representative Rhinock or the fraud allegations. It was never really established that the article that set all of this off was even serious; Criswell was a humorist, after all. Would an apology and a retraction have saved a life and a newspaper? Had there ever really been a fraud committed? Had something been overlooked? Had the book simply not been started yet? These questions remain unanswered, and now, more than a century later, history is unlikely to reveal them.

THE STRANGE STORY OF HERBERT S. BIGELOW

Herbert S. Bigelow was born in Elkhart, Indiana, on January 4, 1870. He attended Indiana public schools and then Oberlin College in Ohio. After graduating from Western Reserve University in Cleveland, he moved to Cincinnati in 1894.

He became ordained as a Congregational minister in 1895 and became pastor of the Vine Street Congregational Church in Cincinnati. Bigelow then got into politics; he served as a delegate to the fourth constitutional convention of Ohio in 1912, serving as president. He served as a member of the state House of Representatives in 1913 and 1914.

When World War I began, Bigelow was vocal in his opposition to American entry into the war and to conscription. Many Ohioans considered him unpatriotic or even a traitor to his country. He was viewed as more than a bit controversial. During speeches, he spoke of "A big ole' rousing revolution," terms that did not endure him to his fellow politicians. His name was spoken in whispered shadows.

In October 1917, Bigelow was kidnapped, attacked and severely beaten by several men dressed in Ku Klux Klan outfits, apparently for being a pacifist and socialist. The attack left him bloodied and with several cracked ribs. Bigelow also had a broken collarbone. Though the assailants had tried to kill him, he recuperated. Socialist groups were quick to come to his defense, especially Frank H. Lamonte, socialist candidate for mayor of Evansville, Indiana. H.H. Carson, socialist city chairman, denounced the attack as "dastardly." Regarding the attack, though some defended him, the mayor of Cincinnati, George Puchta, argued that Bigelow received "what's coming to him."

Frederick H. Robinson, editor of *Medical Review of Reviews*, offered a $1,000 reward for information leading to the capture and conviction of those responsible for the kidnapping of Bigelow. In an age when character mattered, Bigelow was seen as a little opaque for some of his political views. He regularly stirred up passionate debate, and most people felt that this was reason enough for the brutal beating.

As Bigelow was recovering, it came to light that there as a full-blown conspiracy to have him killed. A *Cincinnati Enquirer* headline dated October 31, 1917, stated: "Thousand in Secret League That Directed Attack on Bigelow Tis Said!" Plotters were reported to have held a conference.

The article described the demands of the league: that members be loyal to the government and demand that all others do the same. It further described Bigelow's injuries. He had been tied to a tree and horsewhipped by approximately forty men. Ultimately, it was decided that the attack was not a federal crime but a local one. With no evidence to prosecute the anonymous, white-robed kidnappers and attackers, no charges were filed.

After recovering from his attack, Bigelow reentered politics and served on the Cincinnati City Council in 1936. In 1937, he was elected to the Seventy-Fifth Congress and served from January 3, 1937, to January 3, 1939. He lost the election to the Seventy-Sixth Congress in 1939. He came back to local politics as a member of the city council in 1940 and 1941. He also resumed his duties as pastor of the Vine Street Congregational Church.

No reliable records exist as to Bigelow's personal life. No known wife or children are on record, although some claim he had a wife.

Bigelow died at the age of eighty-one on November 11, 1951. He remains were cremated, and the ashes were scattered over his farm in Forestville in Shelby County. Whatever secrets he held, personal or political, he carried them to the grave. Herbert S. Bigelow remains a mysterious figure in Cincinnati.

9

GEORGE "BOSS" COX

CITY BOSSES AND THE SILENT GRIP ON POWER

Political corruption is nothing new. It has been around, in one form or another, since before the Greeks invented governments as we know them today.

During the nineteenth and early twentieth centuries, leaders known as "city bosses" routinely assumed domineering control over city politics. They did not gain power through the established procedure of campaigning and election to office by the people. These bosses muscled their way into power through criminal means. They used tactics such as blackmail and bribery to control elected public officials. The bosses would then grant these public officials favors if they cooperated. While some bosses reigned over nearly all the city, some operated in a single neighborhood. Sometimes, more than one boss competed for control over an area; this often led to mob-style violence. Several of Cincinnati's unsolved murders are thought to be linked to this activity.

One such case stems from a bizarre set of circumstances surrounding an assault and possible murder that had been cleverly concealed. The plot unraveled in May 1890, when a round of gossip reached police headquarters. A cop was at last sent to see if the gossip was anything more than a rumor. Following the vague plot of the gossip, the police sent an undercover agent into Wielert's Cafe on Vine Street. The undercover agent, and an accomplice, said he was a friend of "Wes," the subject of the gossip. He demanded to see him, saying he had been sent by a man named "Boss," who had also been mentioned in the gossip. By 1890, the name "Boss" was one to be cautious about. Begrudgingly, the café's bartender sent the men through the side door and up to the third floor. When they entered, they found an empty room, except for a dirty bed with an obviously wounded man lying on it and a nervous nurse attending him. He was wearing an undershirt badly stained with blood. Curled up in a fetal position, the man seemed too barely be alive. On examination, "Wes" had a large and ghastly wound on the back of his head. His skull was badly fractured to a depth of one inch. Multiple bone fragments could be seen embedded in clumps of dried blood. It appeared that a surgeon had sewn up the wound in a rough manner that was most likely not done in a hospital situation. The men tried to speak with the victim but were only able to get a few disjointed comments during a moment of lucidity. The nurse on call stated, "He had fallen down a flight of stairs and hurt himself." One thing that the man was able to say, in reply to the nurse, was, "I didn't get hit that way." He made no more useful statements. The two men thought that it would be a miracle if the man survived, but he was attended to by medical professionals operating in a criminal capacity. The operative and his partner left to make other inquiries. It was soon learned that Wes was a harness maker who had been seen at a saloon named Dead Man's Corner at the corner of Longworth and John Streets. George "Boss" Cox owned Dead Man's Corner. Thought to be a messenger for Cox, Wes had been in Wielert's Cafe, indiscreetly arguing with an unknown person. When the argument got disruptive, the bartender, Heil, grabbed a beer mallet and struck him on the head.

Dr. McKenzie was brought in to attend the wound. Heil, it turned out, had gone to great effort and expense to keep the affair quiet, perhaps at the request of Cox. When authorities questioned Dr. McKenzie, he stated that he knew nothing of the incident and could elaborate no further. The investigators noted his nervous disposition and felt that there was more to the chain of events than McKenzie was letting on. Given that the whole affair was based on speculation and gossip, no further inquiry could be justified. The chief of police thought there was more to the gossip than just a common bar fight gone wrong. The operative agreed.

The case was dropped. A few days later, a corpse matching the description of Wes, wound and all, was dumped in an alley on the edge of the Miami and Erie Canal. The corpse had no ID on it and was not claimed. The unidentified stiff was buried in an unmarked grave in the pauper's cemetery on the edge of town. It was never determined if the body was that of the mysterious Wes or not. It was also never confirmed if he worked for "Boss"

Cox or not. No one was ever prosecuted in the case of Wes. His identity and purpose are left to the mysteries of history.

Most city bosses ruled with an iron fist. They used whatever means they had, including bribes, assaults, intimidation, and murder. While bosses allowed gambling establishments and prostitution rings to operate as a reward to those that were loyal to them, they also restricted the availability of these items to increase their value to those the bosses granted them to. In this era, city bosses ran towns like Newport, Kentucky.

Good city bosses realized that they needed to maintain a positive public image, even while they acted as dictators behind the scenes. Bosses would often make a big show of charitable work. They would make sure to be seen at festivals and to visit sick children at local hospitals. Some of the bosses realized they could manipulate the levers of power if they had high public approval, so they worked to maintain it. Image was everything. A few city bosses made efforts to do some public good, even if their motives were often selfish. They set out to make improvements in public life during the late nineteenth and early twentieth centuries. At this time, southwest Ohio grew rapidly, with many thousands of new residents moving to towns like Hamilton, Dayton, and Lebanon. Hamilton County was outpacing elected city officials' ability to keep up with the increasing demand for services. Bosses commonly filled the gap in municipal services by having streets swept, garbage removed, night patrols conducted, and other services rendered. They used kickbacks to pay the homeless and the unemployed to do these jobs, thereby creating more loyalty among the people. Those who did the bidding of the bosses were called the "City Machine." Legitimately elected officials were less likely to cross a boss if they didn't know who was in the boss's pockets and who was not.

The most famous and feared city boss of the late nineteenth and early twentieth centuries was George Barnsedale Cox. He grew up working his brother-in-law's keno games, where he learned a lot about gambling and strong-arming. Those running the games needed debts to be paid, otherwise, they looked weak and would be taken advantage of in the next games.

Dead Man's Corner was at the intersection of Longworth and John Streets and was the gateway to Cincinnati's red-light district and the center of power for the notorious Eighteenth Ward. This was where George B. Cox got his start running a saloon on the southwest corner. The saloon taught him how to get away with beating folks up. Cox was elected to the city council in 1879; he served two terms. He became the most powerful member of the Republican Party in Cincinnati by the 1880s. He went on to chair the

Wielert's Café, built in 1873, was the hangout during the heyday of Boss Cox's corruption. It still stands on Vine Street. *Photo by Nancy Heizer.*

Hamilton County Republican Committee by force. Once he became a boss, Cox virtually ran Cincinnati. Like early crime bosses in Chicago and New York, Cox spent lavishly on payoffs and "gifts" to build support for himself among the public in Cincinnati. Cox would then have his followers vote for the candidate he supported, thereby installing his people into government. Cox once stated: "The people do the voting. I simply see that the right candidates are selected." By the late 1800s, if a politician wanted any office in Cincinnati, he had to get Cox's approval. Cox also "required" the politicians he placed in office to appoint those loyal to him to lower-level governmental positions. The Boss Cox regime was the very definition of what we today call pay-to-play. These city positions often included police officers, firefighters, street cleaners, city services, clerks, and numerous others.

He had managed, by 1904, to place nearly every Republican ward chairman in a city position. Few resisted his efforts. To build loyalty and support among the opposition party, Cox also appointed members of those parties to a substantial number of city offices. To show their loyalty to Cox, these appointees had to relinquish 2.5 percent of their salary to the

Hamilton County Republican Committee. He, in turn, used the illegally obtained kickback money to buy future votes. It was kind of a power Ponzi scheme. Though it would eventually lead to his undoing, Cox paid residents of nearby states to come to Cincinnati to vote illegally in close elections. He also had no problem with his loyal voters casting more than one ballot under assumed names, provided the person voted for Cox's candidate. His men would simply pull names out of obituaries and vote under the names of the recently deceased.

By 1905, Cox's domination of Cincinnati government was beginning to show cracks. In 1905, Secretary of War (and Cincinnati native) William Howard Taft delivered a speech in Akron that attacked Cincinnati's corruption under the rule of "Boss" Cox. This speech rallied many in Cincinnati to oppose Cox. Over the next few years, Cox managed to anger some of his political allies. He wanted to implement a plan that they saw as wrong. Many new residents wanted a government free of corruption. They opposed Cox's criminal regime. Many of these people were supporters of the Progressive movement and members of the Charter Party.

Led by Murray Seasongood, the Charter Party (the members were known as Charterites) sought to bring corruption to heel. They sought to return Cincinnati to traditional morals. With an influx of new residents, voters that Cox could not control, he failed to have his candidate elected mayor in 1911. Henry Hunt, a reformer, won the mayoral race that November. City bosses had traditionally maintained their power by guaranteeing their promises to loyal candidates. Cox failed in 1911, and his machine quickly fell apart. His supporters deserted him overnight, and his word meant nothing. In the years after Cox's defeat at the hands of Progressive reformers, he found himself out of power.

George B. Cox died in 1916 following a stroke at his home in Clifton. Built in 1894, his beautiful sandstone home, which was designed by renowned Cincinnati-based architect Samuel Hannaford, was placed in the National Register of Historic Places on November 6, 1973. It is now a branch of the Hamilton County Public Library system. It is open to the public, and many of the house's features are from Cox's time in the home. Over the years, the house has taken on a legacy all its own. Legend says that the home has secret tunnels that run underground to Over-the-Rhine and to Weidmann's Bar, where Cox often spent time and delegated his power.

The new charter-backed legislation passed in 1924. It reorganized the Cincinnati City Council from a thirty-two-member system to a nine-member system, with nonpartisan elections. It created a civil service system

The George "Boss" Cox mansion in Clifton. It looks today much as it did when it was built in 1894. *Photo by Nancy Heizer.*

to eliminate political patronage and made Cincinnati the first large city with a council-manager administration. Most offices in Cincinnati government would either be elected positions or direct hire positions. With the new law in place, Seasongood was overwhelmingly elected to the Cincinnati City Council. Two years later, Murray Seasongood was elected mayor in the 1925 elections. Of course, the election of Seasongood didn't end political corruption, but it did end the city boss system.

10

TRAGEDY AT THE AVERY HOUSE

William Ledyard Avery was an eminent lawyer and judge in the Hamilton County Common Pleas Court. In 1877, he presided over one of the strangest cases in Hamilton County history: *Zeigler v. Bruckman*. The case involved slander over the terms of witchcraft and the occult. After a bizarre trial, Avery eventually ruled that Bruckman had not slandered Zeigler, leaving Zeigler to pay the costs. The Avery family was quite wealthy, and William Avery built a beautiful twelve-room mansion in North Bend (the present-day College Hill neighborhood) in 1850. The estate featured a Rookwood Pottery fireplace, several outbuildings, a large barn, and a working horse farm. The Avery family was quite prominent in Cincinnati in the latter decades of the nineteenth and the first decades of the twentieth centuries, especially in legal and society circles. On February 5, 1878, he married Johanna Ummethun. The couple had a daughter, Ethel, in November of the same year. Just over a year later, they had a son, Coleman W. Avery. He was born on February 22, 1880, in Cincinnati.

Growing up in Cincinnati society, Coleman Avery was educated in the city's public schools. Young Coleman graduated from the University of Cincinnati in 1902. He immediately entered the university's law school and graduated in 1905. Avery married his first wife, Elinor Coates Baer of Baltimore, Maryland, in 1904. Coleman was admitted to the Ohio Bar later in 1905. A newly licensed lawyer, Avery joined Cincinnati's Honest Elections Committee. This was during the reign of George "Boss" Cox, and Cincinnati was drowning in political corruption. A Democrat who

The Avery mansion in College Hill. Built in 1850, this magnificent structure was the boyhood home of Coleman Avery. *Photo by Nancy Heizer.*

vowed to fight Cox's corrupt political machine, Avery was appointed to the Honest Election Committee's executive committee.

On July 1, 1907, the Averys welcomed a baby boy, John Coleman, into the family.

In 1909, Avery was appointed a Hamilton County assistant prosecutor by Henry T. Hunt; this was Avery's first public office and would prove to be a catalyst for a professional legal career. Over the next three years, Avery's position brought him into conflict with Boss Cox on numerous occasions.

Avery was, in 1912, named an assistant city solicitor. He held this position for two years. In 1914, against the backdrop of World War I, he ran an unsuccessful campaign for election to the bench for the Hamilton County Court of Common Pleas, a seat his father had held for a decade. After his defeat, Avery entered private practice beginning in 1915. He then accepted a faculty position at the Cincinnati Law School teaching night classes from 1916 to 1918. During these years, Avery served as Special Assistant District Attorney for War. He worked out of the Cincinnati office of the United States Attorney for the Southern District of Ohio. This afforded the affable and tenacious Avery a chance to become a prominent Cincinnatian in his own right. During World War I, Avery served as a major in the Second Battalion for the Cincinnati Home Guards.

In 1919, just as the Spanish influenza pandemic was spreading across Cincinnati, Avery returned to private practice. On June 10, 1920, he was appointed to the Ohio Supreme Court by Governor James M. Cox (no direct relation to George "Boss" Cox, who had passed away in 1916). Avery replaced Justice Stanley Merrell, who had resigned to accept a position as the lead counsel for Cleveland, Cincinnati, Chicago, and St. Louis Railway Corporation.

Justice Avery's short tenure on the Ohio Supreme Court saw him write four majority opinions. In his decision in the case of *Smith v. Smith*, the case dealt with whether the secretary of the state of Ohio performed an illegal act when certifying the names of candidates to appear on primary election ballots. It also dealt with questions of whether Ohio common pleas and appellate courts held the authority to review the secretary of state's actions. Justice Avery, in writing for a unanimous court, ruled that Ohio's courts properly exercised their authority when deciding if election officers used appropriate measures or engaged in fraudulent or corrupt activities.

Further, Justice Avery found that sections of the Ohio General Code limited election officers' discretion in determining candidates' eligibility as to whether the candidates were registered electors who were eligible to seek offices. Justice Avery, on behalf of the Ohio Supreme Court, granted a peremptory writ of mandamus ordering the Secretary of State for Ohio, Harvey V. Smith, to place the name of Harry Clay Smith on the Republican primary election ballot for the office of secretary of state.

In the early twentieth century, as today, Ohio Supreme Court seats were publicly elected positions for a two-year term. In November, six months after his appointment, Avery stood for election to the state's highest court for a full two-year term. He lost his bid for election to World War I veteran and Ohio adjutant general Benson M. Hough.

After his unsuccessful run for election in November 1920, Justice Avery returned to Cincinnati from Columbus to resume private practice. He also began to lecture on criminal law at the Cincinnati YMCA Law School. Between 1908 and 1921, the Averys had added four more children to their family. In the 1920s, there were many clubs and organizations around Cincinnati, several of which Avery was an active member of. He was involved with the Duckworth Democratic Club as well as the Miami Valley Hunt and Polo Club. The bridle paths at Winton Woods Park, which are still used to this day, were furthered by Avery on behalf of the Hunt and Polo Club. On May 22, 1928, Elinor Avery passed away due to complications from tuberculosis. As was proper in the early twentieth century, Justice Avery went into mourning for a year. At the conclusion of his mourning period, he resumed the practice of law, taking cases from across the eastern United States.

Throughout his career, Avery invested in commercial real estate in Cincinnati. Along with his sister Ethel, he bought several properties, which they then rented for a return on their investment. One of his properties, the Commercial Arts Building, was where he maintained the offices for his law practice. While the buildings he owned were quite valuable, by late 1929, the Great Depression had hit America. Businesses and shops that had occupied his buildings closed and vacated the premises. His rent-producing properties were all but empty. The income from remaining tenants barely covered taxes and mortgages. His private practice's caseload was also significantly reduced, as the public had no disposable income to hire lawyers. His financial situation began to be a struggle, and those around Avery began to note a shift in his personality. He was transitioning from a gregarious fellow to a grumpy recluse. Colleagues also noticed that the previously teetotaling lawyer had become an occasional drinker, sometimes to excess. Despite a shift in mood, Avery continued to work assiduously at his law practice. An avid outdoors and animal enthusiast, Avery continued to breed and raise Irish terriers. Working with the horses on his estate continued to occupy his time and devotion.

One of his cases took him to Lynchburg, Virginia. There, he began to court Sarah Loving. The couple was married in 1934. Sarah became stepmother to Coleman's five children; the couple had no children of their own. During this time, Avery began to represent a man named A. Willis Hunter. Hunter was involved in a civil suit against the Oldroyd Machine Company. Originally formed in Delaware, the company had acquired property in Cincinnati and operated under the name Oldroyd Mining Company. The case embroiled Avery, and it dragged on for more than a year. By this time, Avery, fighting depression and an increasing struggle with alcoholism, became obsessed with the case. He was sure that his client was in the right and that he would see the case resolved in his favor for a judgment of $100,000. Somewhere between obsessive and tenacious, Avery sank his own money into the case, going so far as to sell off assets to cover his expenses. He was not being paid a salary for his work while the case was ongoing, in lieu of a settlement at the conclusion of the case. He eventually won the case against Oldroyd, but it filed for bankruptcy and was shielded from having to pay the award to Hunter. He found that he was unable to collect the judgment. He was also unable to collect his fees of nearly $35,000. The Oldroyd case left him in financial straits and emotional melancholy.

Financial pressures on Avery began to mount. His inability to collect the judgment awarded to him and the associated legal fees, the ongoing ramifications from the Great Depression and quarrels with Sarah all weighed on his mind. The once-proud lawyer and Ohio Supreme Court justice soon needed to be hospitalized for depression. In the 1920s and '30s, any such institutionalization would result in a collapse of social standing and professional reputation. Amid his forlornness, Avery had a minor heart attack. He recuperated, but the attack left him even more worried. According to friends and family, he began to drink more heavily than ever.

On more than one occasion, neighbors across the street reported hearing shouting and items breaking. By the early thirties, Avery was a full-blown alcoholic. His developing addiction was a stunning twist, given that, at this time, America was under Prohibition and the sale of alcohol was strictly illegal. In Cincinnati during Prohibition, a fellow lawyer and associate of Avery's named George Remus became known as "King of the Bootleggers." Remus built a bootlegging empire and made himself a fortune dealing in illegal booze. In all likelihood, Avery purchased his liquor from Remus. He would hide whiskey bottles in various places around the property, mostly in the barn. Avery and Remus were to share a somewhat similar fate as history unfolded. Prohibition was at last repealed on December 5, 1933, and liquor was once again legal in America. A few blocks west of Avery's mansion, at the corner of North Bend and Hamilton Avenue, was his favorite bar. He would drive down to it and drink the evenings away. When Avery returned home, he and Sarah would argue over his drinking and driving. Their arguments were sometimes volatile and occasionally resulted in minor domestic violence on both of their parts, he in a drunken stupor, she in an angry rage. Worried about, and angry with, her husband, Sarah would have a family friend, Jack Haskin, follow Avery to the bar and remove his distributor cap, disabling the vehicle. Avery, unable to start his car, would stumble home down the sidewalk. The next morning, Haskin would replace the cap and drive the car to Avery's mansion. In the middle of this, his first-born son, John Coleman Avery, passed the Ohio Bar and joined his father in private practice in 1935. The two worked together, even though by 1935 the American economy had barely recovered from the Great Depression.

As the latter half of the 1930s dawned, things slowly got worse for Avery. He was now drinking to excess daily. His legal work had slowed to a trickle, and his behavior had irreparably damaged his reputation around Cincinnati. Along with alcoholism, he continued to struggle with depression. His family and friends were becoming more and more concerned with his state of being. Father and son, although they worked in the same office, barely spoke. Avery was spending all his time either hiding in the barn drinking or fighting with Sarah. The dogs and horses were neglected. He was forced to sell several of his properties to pay bills, therefore reducing his overall income. Lawyer work was essentially nonexistent.

Around the summer of 1937, he began to gamble in an effort to reverse his financial fortunes. Gambling quickly proved to make matters worse. He lost several of his horses and went further into debt. The gamblers he was associating with put him at odds with his profession, as much of it was illegal. The winter of 1937–38 was a long, cold one for Cincinnati, and snow fell in record amounts. Conditions left Avery unable to get downtown to his office or to solicit more cases. Sarah was almost constantly concerned with his well-being.

The family was barely making ends meet. Their once enviable collection of art and furniture was down to a few paintings and the basic furnishings necessary to run a proper house. Thursday, March 10, 1938, was an unusually warm day in Cincinnati. Temperatures hovered in the mid-forties. The weather was mild, and the Averys' neighbors across the street were on their porch when they heard a loud argument from the other side of the road. They looked up to see Coleman chasing Sarah across the yard with a baseball bat, screaming obscenities and threats. Later that day, the neighbors went to check on Sarah and found her knitting in the living room. All seemed calm.

It all came to a dramatic and terrifying conclusion on the morning of Monday, March 14, 1938. As the sun broke on the eastern horizon, Sarah got up early to do some housework. A little after 9:00 a.m., she was cleaning strawberries at the kitchen sink. Coleman quietly crept into the kitchen and came up behind his wife. He pressed a loaded, double-barreled shotgun against the back of her head. He pulled the trigger. With a loud bang, he splattered her brains all over the kitchen cabinets and counter. Three windowpanes were shattered by buckshot, and blood was sprinkled on the glass that remained intact. The window frame was covered in pellets and blood. Sarah's entire face was ripped off by the violent impact of the shotgun blast. Fragments of blood, brains, and tissue were all over her hands and apron. She died instantly, slumping to the floor, where she continued to bleed. Her juice-soaked knife and a few fresh strawberries fell to the floor with her.

No one knows how long Coleman Avery stood over his wife's dead body before putting the shotgun under his own chin and pulling the trigger. The blast came out of the back of his head and threw brains and buckshot all over the other side of the kitchen. It managed to leave most of his jawbone and face intact, but the back of his skull was completely gone. One ear was left dangling from a slim piece of muscle tissue. Upon impact, his knees buckled, and he fell sideways onto the floor just longways from Sarah's corpse. Blood splattered and ran across the tile floor. The smell of gunpowder and fresh fruit smoldered in the air. Their manservant, George Mosley, was standing on the porch of his cottage behind the main house, drinking his morning coffee. He heard the two blasts and went to investigate. He entered the house and followed the smell to the kitchen. On entering the kitchen, he saw the carnage before him. He nearly fainted. Mosley saw the two corpses lying in a pool of their mingled blood. The police and the coroner were called in, and an investigation ensued. It was evident from the scene what had happened. A few witness accounts of the Averys' quarreling and financial struggles and Coleman's alcoholism closed the case as a murder-suicide. Mosley later stated to the coroner that the scene was so messy that he couldn't tell the difference between the strawberry juice and blood. No one alive would be held legally responsible.

On March 16, 1938, a private funeral was held for Coleman W. Avery. He was laid to rest in peace at Spring Grove Cemetery later same day. The Loving family of Virginia did not want their beloved Sarah to be buried with her murderous husband. They requested that her body be sent back to Virginia for burial at Spring Hill Cemetery in Lynchburg. She was only forty-six years old. The Averys left behind five children: John Coleman, Ledyard, Elinor Louise, Mary Frances and Elizabeth Coates "Eliza" Avery. John Coleman Avery moved to Covington, Kentucky, to avoid direct association with his father. He continued to practice law in Kentucky for the remainder of his career. The Avery estate was sold off and is now in private ownership.

LIBBY HOLMAN, ACTRESS OR MURDERESS?

Elizabeth Lloyd Holzman was born May 3, 1904, in Cincinnati to parents Alfred and Rachel Holzman. Early in her life, her wealthy family became destitute after Holman's uncle, Ross Holzman, embezzled nearly $1 million of the family's stock brokerage business. Alfred then altered the family name to Holman, presumably to hide their Jewish identity and to avoid the scandal.

Elizabeth began her career starring in University of Cincinnati musical productions, but she soon moved to New York City. The vivacious young woman was headed for Broadway. Holman soon developed a following as a chanteuse act with her song "Body and Soul."

Holman's Broadway debut was in the play *The Sapphire Ring* in 1925. She did well on Broadway, getting good reviews in several shows. She continued to have success and made her film debut in 1947's *Dreams That Money Can Buy*, but it turned out to be her only film role. Her fashion style began to gain attention, and she began to be known for wearing strapless dresses, a style she is credited with inventing.

Soon, though, she began to get more attention for her lifestyle off the stage and screen than on. She soon made headlines due to a relationship with Louisa Carpenter, an heiress to the DuPont fortune. It was the first lesbian relationship to be openly followed by the media. The sensational affair quickly changed the direction of her career. The press still clamored for her attention, but not to ask about her latest Broadway review.

Portrait of Libby Homan at the height of her public popularity. *Photo in public domain.*

When her relationship with Carpenter fell apart, she married Zachary Smith Reynolds of the famous Reynolds tobacco family from North Carolina on November 29, 1931. On July 5, 1932, Libby and Smith held a party for their friend Charles Gideon Hill Jr. at Reynolda, their Winston-Salem home. It was just after midnight on July 6, 1932, when a shot was heard in the home. Smith Reynolds had been murdered, shot in the head with a Mauser .32 pistol. Although the circumstances of the murder were mysterious, Holman was arrested for the crime. During the investigation, she was found to be pregnant with their child. Investigative interviews revealed that Smith's personal assistant, Albert Bailey "Ab" Walker, had found Smith unconscious after hearing Libby scream, "Smith's shot himself." Walker then moved Smith and altered the scene. He removed Smith from the house and took him to the hospital, where he died early that morning. Walker was also questioned during the investigation. Rumor had it that Holman and Walker were involved in an affair. Holman's lawyers argued that it was suicide, but that was never officially established. The investigation was a field day for the press; sensational headlines made national newspapers. Holman was released from custody and the charges were dropped; many people thought that it was due to the Reynolds family's influence and their considerable fortune. No one was ever brought to trial over the murder of Zachary Smith Reynolds.

Later, Libby married again, this time to Ralph Holmes. This marriage did not last. They separated after just over five years, mostly spent apart due to his military service during World War II. Ralph Holmes was found dead from a barbiturate overdose before divorce proceedings could take place. Her son Christopher Smith "Topper" Reynolds died in 1950 at the age of seventeen in a questionable "accident" while mountain climbing. Her personal life was in shambles, and her professional career began to suffer as a result.

Holman was doing little stage work by this point, but she was still making headlines over her personal life. She took one more shot at marriage on December 27, 1960, when she wed renowned artist Louis Shanker. He was an Orthodox Jew, and the couple practiced Judaism in the home, something Holman had not done in years. He did not allow her homosexual friends to visit their home, which led to her resenting him. Their marriage was strained, but the couple never officially divorced. A few years later, in 1966, her lover Montgomery Clift died suddenly and unexpectedly. By this time, she had mostly withdrawn from the spotlight.

She continued her lifelong work of supporting charities and the civil rights movement.

On June 18, 1971, she put on a bathing suit, went to her garage and got into her Rolls Royce. She started the engine and sat there as exhaust fumes filled the garage. The iconic entertainer, after years of headlines and scandals, had committed suicide. She saved the most dramatic headline for last.

12
ANNA MARIE HAHN

Anna Marie Filser was born in Fuessen, Germany, on July 7, 1906. She was the youngest of twelve children, and her family was devout Catholics. They were also of some means and standing in Fuessen society. At all times, a robust set of beliefs were to be abided by and a strict set of rules followed. By all accounts, her childhood was normal.

When Anna was seventeen years old, however, she began a relationship with a Viennese doctor. A short time later, she became pregnant, and when she informed him, he revealed that he was a married man. The doctor suggested that she have an abortion, but as Anna was a devout Catholic, this was out of the question. Their relationship ended, and Anna was on her own. Upon learning that Anna was having a child out of wedlock, her family sent her to Holland to live with a sister until she gave birth. It was quite common in those days for unwed, expectant mothers to be sent away to give birth, in order to hide the pregnancy from a judgmental society.

She had a baby boy she named Oskar in late 1925. After he was born, she returned to Germany but soon found that the gossip and slander about her marital status with a baby was unacceptable. She ill endured people's looks and stares and the innuendos and questions. Filser soon wrote to an uncle in Cincinnati and asked if she could come to America. The uncle, Max Doeschel, agreed to help her emigrate. Anna Marie Filser arrived in America on February 12, 1929.

In 1929, Cincinnati was a bustling city with a large German population. There were several German-language newspapers and many German societies. Over-the-Rhine and other parts of Cincinnati were filled with German language and culture. A young German woman would not have raised any suspicions at all, and she would have no trouble finding work. Her first job here was as a housekeeper in a hotel. She also found Cincinnati to have an active German social network. It wasn't long before she was going to dances and gatherings. At one of these dances, she met a nice young man by the name of Philip Hahn. They began to "step out," and before long, they were in a regular relationship. She was up front with Philip about having a son back in Germany. He took it in stride, and a proposal was imminent. She agreed to the marriage when he agreed to allowed her to bring her son to live in their home.

Anna Marie Hahn, as she appeared in court. *Courtesy of Vocal.Media.*

Their engagement was brief, and they married in Buffalo, New York, on May 5, 1930. She was now Anna Marie Hahn. Two months later, she traveled to her native Germany to get six-year-old Oskar and bring him to live with her in America. The couple started a restaurant and a bakery in Cincinnati, but both failed due to the stock market crash of 1929 and its long-term effects on the economy. Soon, the Hahn family's luck turned when she inherited the house of a man named Ernest Kohler. He had been a childhood friend of Hahn's father, and when he died in 1933, he left the house and furnishings to the Hahn family. Real estate records indicate that the house was valued at a little over $12,000.

Even though the Hahns had a house, their financial future looked bleak. Philip was still out of work, and by then, Anna had become a housewife, tending to her husband and son. To help the family financially, Anna began to gamble. In the early 1930s, Newport, Kentucky, was a hot spot for gambling. Small casinos were set up on nearly every corner. Bets were wagered, and money flowed. A horse race was never hard to find, and folks bet on them as ardently as they did at the casino tables. Anna began to visit the tracks regularly, betting sums of money that were scraped together and borrowed.

Anna was an attractive woman with an exotic-sounding European accent; she quickly found that she could get the attention of financially secure men. Realizing that she could, with a few words of flattery, manipulate powerful, wealthy men was a revelation for her. In many ways, it changed the trajectory of her life, and several other lives as well. One of these men was George Heis. He was a coal merchant, and she borrowed large sums of money from him to support her gambling addiction. In 1936, his creditors demanded that he pay his debts, and he demanded she pay hers. Of course, Anna didn't have the money to pay back her debts to Heis, so she used her womanly ways to get him to agree to an alternative. She would cook for him. Soon after consuming a meal that she had fixed for him, he became ill. Heis experienced violent vomiting, nausea, strong headaches, and paralysis. He did recuperate, but the illness left him in an altered state, partially paralyzed. With Heis' ability to work now ended, the coal company he worked for came directly to Anna for the money it was owed. She was not able to pay the debt.

Anna Hahn then set her sights on another older man from the German community, Albert Palmer. He was in his seventies and had a modest pension from his years as a railroad watchman. He was enchanted with the flirtatious young woman, and he soon agreed to let her prepare some meals for him in his home. She manipulated him into giving her about $1,500, some of which she used to pay the coal company. Some of the money was used at the casinos and racetracks in Newport. Less than a week after giving Hahn the money, though, Palmer suddenly became ill in a manner similar to that of Heis. Palmer did not recuperate. He died on March 27, 1937, under mysterious circumstances. But despite the suspicious circumstances surrounding his death, authorities did not initially link Heis' illness to Palmer's death. The death was ruled "of unknown causes." No further action was taken. This emboldened Hahn, now desperate for money, to continue a pattern that had so far been successful.

A few weeks later, a man named Jacob Wagner came to Hahn's house and claimed that they were related (per testimony Hahn gave later); Wagner's neighbors disputed this. Wagner was a seventy-eight-year-old former gardener. Hahn went to the apartment house where Wagner resided on June 2, 1937. Wagner mysteriously died the next day from a sudden sickness. Hahn went to Wagner's bank the next morning, carrying a check that had been signed by Wagner and made out to Hahn. She told the bank examiner that she was withdrawing funds to pay Wagner's debts and to settle his estate. She went to court to get permission to enter Wagner's one-room apartment. She was granted permission, and an officer of the court escorted her to the apartment. They took into their possession a will. The will left all of Wagner's estate to Hahn. She had acted in a sane, reasonable manner with

The apartment in Clifton believed to be the home of George Gsellman, and the place where he was poisoned. *Photo by Nancy Heizer.*

officials, and they saw nothing untoward in her actions. She was neither questioned nor under suspicion for the death of Jacob Wagner. Hahn had gotten away with murder—twice. She now was on a maniacal course of killing for profit.

It is unknown whether she was looking for another victim when she met George Gsellman, or whether they met by fateful circumstances. It was July 6, 1937, and Hahn had been coming to see Gsellman in his apartment regularly for a few days. On that day, she cooked Gsellman a meal. He immediately became ill, falling to the ground in a pool of his own vomit. He shook violently and barely made it into bed. He soon died. Once again, no one put the deaths together. No one realized that the three dead men all had meals cooked for them by Anna Marie Hahn just before they died. No one realized that Cincinnati had a female serial killer in their midst.

In late September 1937, Hahn met George Obendorfer, a wealthy cobbler. He was sixty-seven, she was thirty-one. A few days later, she signed a check for $1,000 using Wagner's name. In a slight change to her usual pattern, Hahn left Cincinnati with Obendorfer and her young son, Oskar. The trio headed west to Colorado. They arrived and checked into a hotel. The next evening, Hahn prepared a meal for Obendorfer, after which he suddenly became violently ill. She took him to a hospital in Colorado Springs and told the registration desk that he was a stranger she had been introduced to the prior day. She returned to the hotel, leaving Obendorfer at the hospital on his deathbed. With no one at his side, Obendorfer died alone in the hospital on August 1, 1937.

Hahn returned to Cincinnati with her son. A few days later, Cincinnati detectives got a telegram from authorities in Colorado. They wanted the Cincinnati police to bring in Anna Marie Hahn for questioning in the case of stolen jewels. The valuable stones had been stolen from the hotel in Colorado Springs where she had stayed just a few days prior. Hahn had been run out of the hotel's co-owners' private room. After Hahn checked out, the co-owner of the hotel, a woman, realized that two diamond rings had been stolen from her quarters. She reported the theft to the Colorado Springs police, and they, in turn, contacted the Cincinnati police. In addition, Colorado Springs police realized that a woman named Hahn had brought a desperately sick man to their local hospital and then vanished. It was just too much of a coincidence. Cincinnati police brought in Hahn for questioning. She quickly told authorities that she had indeed been to Colorado with her son. She initially denied being in the company of Obendorfer but suddenly remembered that she had traveled with him. She also said that she had prepared a meal for him at the hotel and that he had gotten sick afterward.

During her interrogation, a detective not connected to the case recognized Hahn by name. Sometime, while Hahn was in Colorado, a local restaurant owner contacted Cincinnati police about the unexplained death of one of their regular patrons, Jacob Wagner. He had come in to eat almost every day, and when he failed to show, he was missed. The restaurant owner told police that he had been in the company of one Anna Marie Hahn just before his untimely death.

At the conclusion of a long interrogation, Hahn was taken into custody and lodged in the Hamilton County jail. Cincinnati police opened an official investigation. They started by questioning Anna's husband, Philip, who had no idea that his wife had gone to Colorado until he found a note she had left him. Philip admitted that he and Anna had argued over a bottle that Oskar had found in the family's basement. Philip surrendered the bottle to the Cincinnati police. He also told investigators that his wife had stolen prescription pads from a local physician and used them to secure poisons such as arsenic from a local drugstore. According to Philip's testimony, Hahn had on at least one occasion sent Oskar to get the prescriptions for her; the pharmacist refused to release the order to such a young boy. Based on the evidence they obtained while questioning the Hahns, police secured a search warrant for the suspects' home. During that search, police discovered a hidden bottle of arsenic. Hahn had the gall to demand that detectives return the bottle to her. It stayed in police custody, as did she. The investigation took on more importance when it came to light that two Cincinnati men, Gsellman and Palmer, with connections to Hahn, had died of identical ailments.

The investigation went on for several weeks.

The state of Ohio finally decided to attempt to prosecute Hahn for one of the deaths, that of Jacob Wagner. The state felt that the evidence in this case was the strongest. Against the defense's protests, the judge in the case allowed the prosecution to reference Hahn's familiarity "with several older men." The prosecution made no secret of their intent to seek the death penalty. From 1803 to 1885, public hangings were the authorized mode of execution in Ohio. From 1885 to 1897, hanging was still the preferred method; a new law stated that they must be carried out in private at the Ohio State Penitentiary in Columbus. In 1897, the electric chair was introduced as the only form of execution in Ohio. It was deemed to be more humane and technologically advanced. The prosecution intended to send Hahn to "the chair."

On October 11, 1937, Anna Marie Hahn went on trial for the murder of Jacob Wagner. She pled not guilty to the crime, and her trial was underway. The prosecution established its case by presenting evidence from medical experts who testified as to the method of Wagner's death. One expert testified that Wagner had died from "A tremendous dose of Arsenic." In addition, the prosecution presented a toxicologist who testified that arsenic likely killed Albert Palmer as well. The prosecution even went so far as to display the vital organs of the two men in court. The organs showed signs of arsenic poisoning. Hahn's purse was also submitted as evidence, given that its fibers contained 35 percent arsenic. This was used to establish that Hahn had carried large quantities of arsenic in her purse, most likely over an extended period. Prosecutors tried to introduce evidence from Colorado, but the judge in the case disallowed this evidence in court. Handwriting experts were called in to testify that Hahn had forged the will of Jacob Wagner. This was to establish a financial motive for the murder. Common to most cases, a motive is almost always necessary to establish guilt. The prosecution felt that it had established motive with the documented financial trail that showed how Hahn had benefited from the crimes.

Meanwhile, the defense tried to excuse the testimony and evidence that had been presented so far.

Perhaps the highlight of the trial came when George Heis came to testify for the prosecution. He was still in a wheelchair due to his imposed paralysis. From his wheelchair, he testified that Hahn had manipulated him out of more than $2,000. He testified that Hahn had told him she would transfer an inheritance to his name if he would cover the tax debt. He further testified that Hahn often fixed his meals and that one evening she served him chicken and spinach she had prepared. Heis testified that he became violently sick and was subsequently paralyzed after eating the meal. He further testified that the spinach had a sweet taste. The prosecution was quick to point out that foods containing arsenic are frequently described as sweet, even if they usually are savory foods. The toxicologist further backed up this claim.

Heis concluded his court appearance by leering directly at Hahn, raising a crooked finger and pointing directly at her. He uttered, "She did this to me."

During the trial, reporters from several publications packed the courtroom and the hallways of the courthouse. Newspapers like the *Cincinnati Enquirer* gave dramatic accounts of the testimony. They described in great detail Hahn's supposed role in the deaths of four elderly German gentlemen and the permanent crippling of another. It was not long before the case gained national attention. Newspapers as far away as Boston and Baltimore ran articles about the sensational murder trial that was unfolding in Cincinnati. One headline from the *Chicago Tribune* nicknamed Hahn "Arsenic Anna." Other papers picked up on the name, echoing it across the country. She was described as "Pretty, but utterly cold" and "Poker-faced." The German community didn't come out to defend her during her two-week trial.

Her case continued to be a media circus. In one instance after another, the press uncovered details of her actions that made their way into the courtroom. Newspapers discovered other possible victims. They scoured hospital and morgue records for any deaths by poison. During this fever, one newspaper found that while caring for a sick woman named Julia Kresckay, Hahn had borrowed $800 from her. When Hahn refused to settle the debt, Kresckay said she would prosecute. While no such legal action is available in the records, Kresckay became paralyzed in the same manner as George Heis.

The more detectives and reporters investigated Hahn, the more they found. It was revealed that seventy-nine-year-old Ollie Luella Koehler had died on August 19, 1937, after eating ice cream that Hahn had given her a few weeks earlier. In a strange twist, detectives investigating the Wagner case found some of Koehler's belongings in Hahn's home. They also found signed documentation that left a "Mrs. A. Filser" (remember, Filser was Hahn's maiden name) as Koehler's power of attorney. Though the Koehler case was never brought to trial, the evidence left no other viable suspect.

The prosecution had offered some ninety-six witnesses. After the prosecution wrapped up its case, the defense mounted a rebuttal. However, the defense offered only three witnesses: a toxicologist, Anna Hahn and Oskar. The defense's toxicologist was brought in from Chicago. He argued that the victims' symptoms could well be attributed to many reasons other than arsenic poisoning. He offered age and natural causes as reasons just as likely as poison.

Twelve-year-old Oskar was put on the stand to testify that he had never seen his mother put anything suspicious in Obendorfer's meals. He further testified that some of the bottles discovered in the house may have come from his chemistry set. Many little boys in this era had home chemistry sets. Unfortunately for Anna, he also testified that he and his father had found a bottle of arsenic in the basement that did not belong to him. His contradictory statements did nothing to prove her innocence. At her insistence, Hahn took the stand in her own defense. She testified under oath that Palmer was like a father to her. She even went so far as to present letters they had exchanged in which she described him as a father figure. Hahn claimed her innocence and accused the long list of prosecution witnesses of not telling the truth. Her testimony did little to persuade the jury of her innocence.

The defense finished its case on the afternoon of November 5, 1937. Later that evening, the jury, made up of one man and eleven women, received the case. That night, a Friday, they deliberated for an hour. The next morning, the jury deliberated for more than two hours. They pored over the evidence and recalled testimony. Before lunch, they reached a verdict.

Once the jury had been reassembled in the jury box, and with everyone anxiously awaiting an outcome, the jury foreman stood to announce the verdict: guilty, without mercy (the "without mercy" clause meant that Hahn was eligible for the death penalty). The judge immediately needed to silence the courtroom, which was packed with reporters. Once order was restored, he asked Hahn to stand. In her typical stoic frame, Hahn stood in front of the judge as he passed down the sentence: death by electrocution. She was escorted out of the courtroom, past the clamoring reporters and other onlookers. She walked firmly until she reached the elevator, where she broke down lugubriously. It was later reported that when she made it back to her holding cell, she fainted. The newspapers had a free-for-all regarding her reaction. She was, at least at that moment, the most notorious woman in America.

The defense quickly filed paperwork for a new trial. It cited errors in Hahn's first trial, but the judge denied the appeal. He wrote, "The evidence was so overwhelming that no verdict other than guilty could have been reached by the jury." The Ohio Supreme Court, as well as the U.S. Supreme Court, refused to hear the case of *Ohio v. Hahn*. It seemed that Ohio governor Martin Davey was the only person who stood between Hahn and the electric chair. He was known to oppose the death penalty, and he granted her a clemency hearing. Her attorneys and Oskar asked for leniency. In an unusual move, Davey refused to intervene in the case. He cited the "cold-blooded, so deliberately planned and executed" actions of Hahn as his reason for letting the court's decision stand.

From the time of the trial until the evening of her execution, Hahn consistently stated that she was innocent. However, about an hour before her execution, Hahn gave some revealing letters to her legal team. In the letters, she confessed to the murders. She gave details and stated that things had unfolded almost exactly as the prosecution claimed. Among the lines in her confession letters are the following: "I don't know how I could have done the thing I did in my life; only God knows what came over me when I gave Albert Palmer, that first one, the poison that caused his death. Up in Heaven, there is a God who will judge me. He will know, and he will tell me how it all came about. He will tell me what caused me to do the same things to Mr. Wagner, Gsellman, and the last one, Mr. Obendorfer." She also wrote, "slipped some poison in the oysters."

Hahn went to the electric chair at the Ohio State Penitentiary in Columbus just after 8:00 p.m. on December 7, 1938. The newspapers described her as "a pitiful, whimpering creature" at her arrival at the death chamber. According to those present, as she was led into the chamber, she begged the warden, "don't let them do this to me." Witnesses say that in the middle of her reciting the Lord's Prayer, the executioner threw the switch, making Anna Marie Hahn the first woman in Ohio history to be executed in the electric chair. She was also Ohio's first female serial killer.

While the victims who died from arsenic poisoning are well known, Anna Marie Hahn left two more, often overlooked, victims: her husband, Philip, and her son, Oskar.

While Cincinnati produced Ohio's first female serial killer, she wasn't the city's only serial killer. The Queen City, as locals often call it, has been home to or hunting grounds for more serial killers per capita than any other city in America. In addition to Anna Marie Hahn and the Dayton Strangler, Cincinnati has also had a long list of murderous repeat offenders. These include the Mill Creek Killer, Julia Higbee, the Cincinnati Strangler, Alfred Knapp, Samuel Little, and Donald "Angel of Death" Harvey. Lest we forget, though technically not a serial killer, the infamous Charles Manson was born in Cincinnati.

13

THE OHIO RIVER FLOOD OF 1937

Cincinnati is in the middle of the eastern half of America, approximately halfway between the East Coast and the Mississippi River and halfway between the Gulf Coast and Canada. Being in the middle often means getting the worst of nature's wrath. Cincinnati can have frigidly cold winters and sweltering hot summers. The city has been known to go so long without rain that the soil dries up and cracks like a maze of miniature gullies. The leaves wither to a crisped and seared appearance. It gets thunderstorms that would excite Dr. Frankenstein and send the fiercest monster cowering to the corner of the room. Snow accumulations can easily top three feet, and snowstorms sometimes last for days. Wildly fluctuating temperatures can bring ice storms that lock everything down, sometimes making it impossible to open even so much as a car door. The winds can howl more ferociously than a hungry wolf; the 1974 tornado outbreak that tore across Salyer Park is proof enough of that. Earthquakes have toppled more than a few buildings in Cincinnati; the dismal cloudy days can seem endless and make one mistakenly think they are in Seattle. The sky can be bright and sunny one second but suddenly turn dark and ominous the next.

Then there is the rain…oh, the rain. It has been known to rain for many days in a row. Cincinnati is sometimes called the "City of Seven Hills," which refers to the seven hills of Rome. Due to the hills and valleys in the city's topography, minor street flooding is common. The Ohio River, which slices through greater Cincinnati and is the sole reason for its founding, overflows its banks from time to time. This is common in and of itself and nothing a Cincinnatian does not take in stride.

A view of the Ohio River flood of 1937. *Courtesy of WCPO-9.*

If anything can be said of Cincinnati that everyone can agree on, it's that there is always an exception to the law of nature. That exception came on January 5, 1937. December 1936 had been an unusually warm month, and when New Year's 1937 arrived, there was no blanket of snow across the city. Temperatures were slightly above freezing, and the skies were gray. The first few days of January brought a chilly rain. At first, nothing seemed abnormal, but the rains persisted for several days, and by January 5, folks began to hope for a break in the weather. The Ohio and its tributaries began to spill over their banks. Ponds and creeks swelled beyond their usual holdings. Radio reports started to come in that the entire length of the Ohio—from where it begins in Pittsburgh, Pennsylvania, to where it flows into the mighty Mississippi—was experiencing unusually high levels. A *Cincinnati Enquirer* headline from the January 8 edition stated, "Ohio Flood Backs Up in Creek." A photo accompanied the article, giving Cincinnatians their first glimpse of the impending floods.

By January 10, the National Weather Service had issued flood warnings up and down the entire Ohio River Valley. Low-lying areas all over town were flooding. Basements and ravines were quickly taking on water. The rains continued unabated as temperatures hovered above freezing. The *Cincinnati Enquirer* on that day had the headline, "Proposed Flood Control System" and featured a hand-drawn map highlighting at-risk areas. On the eleventh, a cold front swept through the area, causing wet roads, and sidewalks to freeze. This created a whole new set of dangers, a newspaper article warned of the flood continuing. An article on January 14 stated in boldface type, "**River Rising Steadily; To Pass Flood Stage**." At Henderson, Kentucky, the Ohio was expected to crest at forty-two feet, seven feet above flood stage at Dam 48. The January 16 *Cincinnati Enquirer* headline read, "Rise in Ohio River Abates Just Short of Flood Stage; Crest of Flood-Tide Passing."

The water was now at 51.6 feet. Flood stage in Cincinnati is 52 feet. The headline turned out to be wrong. The National Weather Service reported record rainfall along the entire length of the Ohio River. Late on January 16 and into the seventeenth and eighteenth, water crept up over the banks of the Ohio in some places. Street flooding was beginning to be a real problem. People were starting to realize that this was going to be "the big one." Local meteorologist W.C. Devereaux forecast colder temperatures, stating that it would get down to twenty degrees by the next morning. Freezing temperatures in some areas only hampered the situation. The mix of snow and ice must have been miserable. In those days, people still heated their houses with fireplaces and kerosene space heaters, which meant that an unusually high number of fires broke out across the city. Cincinnati had a long and grand history of paid professional firefighters with the latest horse-drawn firefighting equipment at their disposal. The steam apparatus had just been invented and implemented. However, due to the fierce weather, most of them were grounded. The roads were largely impassable, leading to several houses being left to burn to the ground, ironically, despite all the water around. These fires caused many people to become homeless. They even cost a couple people their lives.

Martial law was declared in Evansville, Indiana, when water levels reached fifty-four feet. The declaration was made in order to manage traffic and utility services, but it was also put in force to dissuade criminals who might try to take advantage of the situation to break into businesses that had closed or houses that had been abandoned for higher ground. Unfortunately, police spent more time disrupting criminals than directing traffic. Things were getting out of hand. While martial law was never declared for Hamilton County, the police were out in full force, patrolling for criminal activity. Citizens were asked to be out and about as little as possible. Several jails in the area reported flooding and were thus unable to house those arrested.

As the river rose, streets that had flooded were now completely washed out. Several houses on steep inclines collapsed and washed down hillsides. The continuing rain cost several people their lives. Large numbers of people drowned directly in the floods. Roads washing out and buildings flooding and collapsing cost others their lives.

Citizens rowing down the street during the 1937 Ohio River flood. It cost many lives and millions of dollars in damage. *Courtesy of WCPO-9.*

Gardens that supplied vegetables to places like Findlay Market washed away in the mudslides. Cows, pigs, chickens and other farm animals drowned. Supply chains were disrupted, and food became scarce.

"Two Escape Death at Hamilton When Auto Plunges into Water" was the January 17 headline in the *Cincinnati Enquirer*. While disaster and danger did not affect everyone in greater Cincinnati, it was widespread and affected millions of people. By January 17, most of the basin (what we call downtown today) was flooded; businesses as far back as Ninth Street were directly impacted. Any business that had been directly on the riverfront was utterly gone. The Miami and Erie Canal, which had been abandoned several years earlier and partially converted into a failed subway project, was now flooded. It brought all kinds of muck and debris onto the streets. Cincinnati was, in 1937, one of the largest and most modern cities in America, but its infrastructure was far less advanced than that of a city today. Sewers were more rudimentary. On January 17, Cincinnati must have felt like it was drowning, because it was. The Queen City was in aquatic chaos.

A modern flood of the Ohio River at Cincinnati, for some perspective. *Photo by Roy Heizer.*

On January 18, the *Enquirer* headline read, "Flood Fear Aroused Again. Officials Keep Watch on Rising Ohio River."

Weather reports called for another two feet of water as a steady rain was forecast for the next forty-eight hours. Fears that the entire city would become Atlantis were not unreasonable. The rains kept coming. Reports up and down the length of the Ohio River were that flooding was widespread. From Pittsburgh to Cairo, Illinois, things were getting worse. One of Cincinnati's oldest radio stations, WLW, broadcast weather and related news reports without commercial interruption for days. The U.S. Army Corps of Engineers sent in workers to manage rescue and relief efforts and to repair damaged floodgates and other infrastructure projects. President Franklin Roosevelt sent in workers from unaffected areas to help with the effort. He promised millions in aid to help the Ohio Valley recover. Between January 13 and 25, Cincinnati saw over a foot of rain.

On January 25, the Ohio River gauges recorded water levels at seventy-eight feet. People evacuated as best they could, but many were trapped in place. While some outside help came, many people were on their own. Just downriver in Louisville, the water had risen to fifty-seven feet, setting a record for that city that has yet to be broken. By the twenty-seventh, Louisville was 70 percent underwater.

Folks south of the river in Covington and Newport were no better off than those in Cincinnati. Businesses along the river were completely underwater. The floodwaters had risen almost as high as the decking of the John A. Roebling Suspension Bridge (then called the Cincinnati-Covington Bridge). To make matters worse, the bridge was shut down for safety reasons; this blocked a main supply route. Downtown Covington evacuated to higher ground. As far back as First Presbyterian Church on Montgomery had at least some flooding. Basements and low-lying areas were inundated with uncontrollable water. City officials in Southgate were concerned that soft, water-soaked ground might give way and topple headstones at Evergreen Cemetery. They also feared the water might unearth the graves. Cemetery officials closed and locked the gates to prevent coffins from floating away. Fortunately, this did not happen.

After three weeks of rain and flooding, the Ohio River finally crested at 79.9 feet on January 26. At just shy of 80 feet, the river had gone 25 feet over flood stage. It had been the worst flooding in the history of Ohio. It broke the previous record from 1884 by somewhere between 4 and 9 feet, depending on where you were. It wasn't until February 5 that the worst-hit areas were again below flood stage. Then, around February 7, freezing cold weather set in, hampering the water level's decline. Luckily, February snowfall was light that year. However, it wasn't until the end of February that water levels had receded to pre-flood levels. The people of Cincinnati proved resilient, with many starting to consider how to move forward. But Cincinnati was never the same.

Many homes in the basin and the West End had been destroyed, displacing many well-to-do citizens. On the east side of the basin, a poor, Black neighborhood named Bucktown was especially hard hit. Almost all of Bucktown needed to be razed. It never came back. Already in substandard housing, hundreds of Blacks were left homeless, forced to rent rather than own. What had been Bucktown became "prime" commercial property, eventually the headquarters for household goods company Procter & Gamble. The town of New Richmond, three miles downriver from the public landing, was one of Cincinnati's hardest-hit areas. It was estimated that 90 percent of its buildings and homes were lost. Nearly everyone who lived there became refugees. New Richmond was so severely affected that city officials redesignated the entire community a flood zone. The area has not been a residential zone since then.

A popular amusement park, Coney Island, was completely inundated. Several of the attractions were destroyed, with parts of them found downriver as far away as Paducah, Kentucky. The Alms & Doepke Department store near the Miami and Erie Canal had its first floor flooded, costing the store hundreds of dollars in lost merchandise and repairs. The Times-Star Building had a leaky roof and sustained damage on several of its upper floors. Crosley Field, home of the Cincinnati Reds at that time, was totally awash.

The U.S. Army Corps of Engineers had helped with rescue efforts, and many members stayed to help with the recovery. Municipal engineers and architects were brought into design flood-control measures. New water-management guidelines were drawn up and implemented. Large earth-moving equipment was used to clear debris and shift areas back in place that had experienced mudslides. The spring and summer of 1937 were spent in recovery and rebuilding. The flood of 1937 did more, though, than altering Cincinnati's topography and structural landscape; it also shifted residential areas. Many citizens of means did not return to the basin. They moved to higher ground, to neighborhoods like Mount Adams, which became an affluent area in the wake of the flood. Areas that had been previously stable, working-class neighborhoods were now decimated and abandoned. Several large churches, including Mother of God in Covington, saw their membership decline as folks moved farther out into the suburbs, away from the river. These shifts in demographics can still be noted today. It was several years before downtown Cincinnati fully recovered.

In total, more than 380 people died (not all of those in Cincinnati) directly from the flooding. Approximately 1,000,000 people were left homeless. The damage was estimated to be $500,000,000. It remains the worst flooding disaster in Ohio history.

14

BREAD OR BULLETS

THE RAWSON MURDER CASE

Over its 233-year history, Cincinnati has been known by several nicknames: the Queen City, the City of Seven Hills, the Nati and Dixie's End. While these names are eloquent descriptions of our fair city, none quite captures the gritty underbelly of the city's industrial heart quite like the apt moniker "Porkopolis."

Throughout the nineteenth century, pork packing was the breadbasket of the Cincinnati economy. Legend has it that so much pork meat was packed in Cincinnati that swine flowed like wine through the streets (most people doubt that this was literally true). Pork packing made many a local man wealthy and kept thousands employed. In the 1800s, pork ruled Porkopolis.

Oddly enough, one of the wealthiest pork-packing barons in Cincinnati was a Jewish man by the name of Elias Kahn. Pork barons like Kahn helped supply a small but successful Cincinnati grocery store started by Cincinnatian Bernard Kroger. Now, more than a century and a half later, one can still buy Kahn's Meat in the deli section at Kroger. One of Elias Kahn's contemporaries was another pork baron by the name of Warren Rawson. He owned and ran the Warren Rawson Pork Packing Company. Along with Elias Kahn, Rawson became one of the wealthiest men in Porkopolis' history.

Warren Rawson and his wife, Francis Delphine (née Williams), were the definition of Cincinnati society. They had married in 1865 and frequently made the *Cincinnati Enquirer*'s social column. The couple regularly appeared at high-society functions around town. Any man who wanted to do business in Cincinnati eventually shook Warren Rawson's hand, while any woman who wanted to be in the right circles made sure to meet Francis Rawson, who was often called "Fanny" by friends and family. They were always listed in *The Blue Book of Cincinnati Society*, a yearly publication of who's who in polite society. The Rawsons had eight children in all (three of whom are directly involved in this story), one boy and seven girls. As was fashionable at the time, the couple bought a beautiful home in the quiet, upscale neighborhood of Clifton, at 444 Warren Avenue. Known as the "Gaslight District," Clifton was the place to own a home if you were a wealthy businessman in the second half of the nineteenth century.

The Rawsons had familial connections to Michigan, and they visited there somewhat regularly. It was on one of these visits, on July 12, 1898, that Warren Rawson died from heart failure. He was only fifty-six years old. He was buried in a prominent place in Spring Grove Cemetery. Warren left a widow, Francis D. Rawson, and eight grown children, as well as a fortune. Francis would never have to work and would be able to sustain her financial position.

The Rawson mansion in Clifton. One of Cincinnati society's most infamous murders unfolded here. *Photo by Nancy Heizer.*

While most of the Rawson daughters were or shortly would be married, two of Fanny's daughters would remain unwed. These two daughters, Nina and Josephine, would remain in the family home with Fanny. Less than five years after her father's death, Deborah married, at the age of twenty-five, a grain mill operator named Vinton Perin. The couple tied the knot on June 3, 1902. It seems that there was some level of stress or tension between Vinton Perin and Fanny almost from the start. Later testimony revealed that the two never clicked and that the trouble started when Vinton failed to ask Francis Rawson for her permission to marry her daughter. When Perin went to probate court to get a marriage license, he was told that he would need his mother-in-law's maiden name, which he did not know. When he called Fanny and asked for her maiden name, she was terse, asking what he wanted it for. She said that she thought it was a peculiar request. She abruptly said, "Williams" and hung up. According to Perin, Mrs. Rawson would not speak to him at the wedding. The precise level of enmity seems to have been lost to time.

Vinton Perin was from Campbell County, Kentucky, just over the river from Cincinnati. He and his brother Lyman were in business together. The two men owned and ran a flour mill based in Cincinnati and had operations in Indianapolis. It was no secret that the Perin Brothers' Milling Company was struggling. Vinton earned a meager living and was not nearly as successful as Warren Rawson; this surely added to the tension between himself and his mother-in-law. Vinton was a hard worker and dedicated to the milling business. Still, he lacked the acumen of Lyman, who appeared to be the better businessman. While Vinton was not winning any businessman of the year awards, tenacity and dedication have their place, and the business of milling flour continued.

For the next twenty years, Vinton and Deborah were happily married. Their marriage produced two boys, Edward and Vinton Jr. By all accounts, they were a happy family. Deborah Perin remained close to her mother and sisters. She frequently visited the family home and socialized. She continued to make the rounds at society events and regularly appeared in the social column of the *Enquirer*. Vinton and Fanny continued to annoy each other.

All seemed relatively well until 1919, when the Perin brothers' business began to fall apart. On April 21, they filed suit in superior court against the Felss Flour Milling Company. The lawsuit regarded a contract for $1,043.15 made by the Felss Company. The Perin brothers claimed that the Felss Company, on February 18, 1918, agreed to purchase 1,000 bags of corn flour at one hundred pounds each—$6.10 per bag. According to court records, the Felss Company accepted 327 bags out of 1,000. The Perin brothers were then forced to sell the remaining 673 bags for $4.55 a bag, for a loss of $1,043.15. The Cincinnati Grain & Hay Exchange had previously investigated the deal and suspended Theobald Felss from the G&H Exchange until the claim by the Perin brothers was settled. Theobald Felss, a longtime member of the chamber of commerce and a traction board member, was furious. The Felss Flour Milling Company took the suspension to the common pleas and appellate courts. A judgment was rendered that the exchange could suspend or expel members as it saw fit. It was further judged that the courts could hold no sway over the claim amount, which led to the suit filed by the Perin brothers. While the claim was eventually settled, it left resentment on the part of Theobald Felss and bad feelings in the milling business community. The Perin brothers had disagreed on certain aspects of the suit, and friction between them began to show.

It was just two years later that Lyman Perin wanted to dissolve the Perin Brothers Milling Company partnership. Documents to dissolve the company were filed in common pleas court. On the day of the hearing, Lyman and Vinton Perin got into a fistfight at the Hamilton County Courthouse. No charges were filed, but it left animosity between the two brothers. They went their separate ways, literally and figuratively. Vinton went east for a time, while Lyman went into business as Perin-Brouse-Skidmore Grain and Milling Company. Soon, though, Vinton came back and attempted to start a milling operation of his own in Indianapolis.

Though he had some connections in Indianapolis from his days with Perin Brothers, Vinton was hard-pressed to find folks who would invest in his mill. He sank what money he had into securing a building and getting some equipment set up. His new mill would be at Emerson Street and Pendleton Pike. He quickly used up what savings he had and found himself strapped for funds to get the operation up and running. Perin spent the next two years trying to pull together the things that were necessary to obtain a functioning mill. With each failure, he became more frustrated. Financial worries were almost continuously on his mind. He went to his sister-in-law for help with the funds, but she stated that she had just purchased a house and that her money was tied up in that investment. According to reports, there was still food on the table, but Vinton was worrying more and more about the mill and his financial woes. He asked Fanny for financial assistance on several occasions, but she refused. However, she began to worry about her daughter's living conditions and the welfare of her two grandsons. During the Perin family financial crisis, Fanny did purchase an apartment house for her daughter.

The idea was that the Perins could live upstairs and rent the lower rooms to University of Cincinnati students. Fanny thought that this would enable her daughter to support the family until Vinton could get some financial stability through the mill. According to later testimony, Nina and Josephine realized that the thought of his wife doing menial labor enraged Vinton. He thought that being a landlady was beneath her dignity, and he wanted to support his wife while she continued to be a housewife and mother to his boys.

Several more weeks passed, and the summer of 1924 was over. Shorter days brought cooler weather, the autumnal equinox was marked off the calendar and fall began. Throughout the day of September 26, Vinton Perin was agitated. He was obsessively worried about money, fearing his mill operation in Indianapolis would fail to launch. As evening neared, Perin told his wife that he was going to Indianapolis to inspect his new mill. As he was leaving, he turned back and called to his younger son, Vinton Jr., saying that he would never see him again because he was going to Indianapolis. It was an ominous statement for a father to make to his son. This, of course, alarmed Deborah, who was already worried about him. As he neared the front door, she said to him, "Do not do anything you might regret. Remember, you have two sons who have to carry your name throughout their lives."

The couple had owned two cars, but due to financial difficulties the previous two years, they no longer had them. Vinton Perin left his wife, his boys and his house in Norwood and stepped onto a streetcar. He wore a brown suit, a brown overcoat, and an Alpine hat, and he carried an alligator-skin case. When the streetcar went around the corner, Deborah Perin began to weep. No one is quite sure what happened in the next hour or two, but Vinton did not head straight to Indianapolis. Instead, he went to his mother-in-law's home in Clifton.

The evening of September 26, 1924 had arrived. That evening, Fanny Rawson and two of her daughters, Nina, fifty-two, and Josephine, forty-six, were in the library socializing and reading.

When Vinton Perin arrived at the Rawson mansion, he was let in by his sister-in-law Nina. He asked to see his mother-in-law and was shown to the library. Fanny was in her usual chair, reading a book, *The Evil Shepard*. Nina stayed in the library with them while Josephine and a housekeeper were in the other room beyond a curtain. Josephine later testified that she did not see Vinton when he first entered the house but recognized his voice from the other room. Without pleasantries, he began to demand money. He first addressed Nina, stating, "Nina, I want money." She replied that she had recently bought a house and that because of that she had no money available. He said he needed money to get "on his feet." He angrily stated that he did not like the idea of his wife doing menial work as a landlady. He reportedly shouted, "You are trying to make my wife a slave to a bunch of bum college students, now I need financial help, and if you don't help me, I will cause a scandal." He continued, "You want her to do menial work, and I will not let her do it." Nina asked what he meant by "scandal," and at that, he drew a pistol and began to fire. He first shot Nina, wounding her slightly. He then turned the gun on his mother-in-law and shot her once in the chest. Perin then turned the gun back to Nina and shot her a second time, this round going into her shoulder. He turned the gun back on Fanny and fired at her again as she sat slumped in her lounge chair. He fired one more shot, this time at Nina, hitting her in the wrist. Nina shouted to her sister to run.

The housekeeper, Miss Schuelter, was clearing dishes from the dining room table when the argument began. She ran from the house when the shots were fired. She ran into the back yard and hid behind a woodpile, fearing for her life. Soon after Schuelter ran from the house, Josephine followed. She ran across the lawn to a neighbor's house, the home of University of Cincinnati professor Guy A. Tawney. Once there, she broke down in a fit of hysteria. She was later taken to the home of her uncle Joseph. While the housekeeper hid behind the woodpile, she witnessed Perin run out the back door of the house and across the lawn in the opposite direction from the one Josephine had taken. He ran into a thickly wooded area just beyond the Rawsons' back yard. He disappeared into the night.

Schuelter later testified that she waited for a few minutes and then returned to the house. She found Nina attempting to pour a glass of water. Nina asked the housekeeper to pour the water for her, because "something terrible had happened." Both Schuelter and Nina returned to the library, where they found Francis Rawson slack in her favorite chair, dead. Though injured, Nina called her uncle, who was the president of the First National Bank. Joseph Rawson Jr. came to the house immediately. As soon as Joseph arrived from his home on Clifton Avenue, he sent for Dr. L.C. Colter. The doctor briefly examined Nina. Aside from shock, he decided that her wounds were not that serious. He sent her to Christ Hospital for treatment. He later removed a bullet from her shoulder and another from her arm just above the wrist.

Police were called, and an investigation was begun. It was twofold, with one unit investigating the crime scene at the house and another searching for the elusive Vinton Perin. Chief of Police Eugene Weatherly contacted Norwood police and asked them to secure Deborah Rawson, wife of the

The grave of Frances D. Rawson in Spring Grove Cemetery. *Photo by Nancy Heizer.*

suspect and daughter of the victim. Norwood police soon brought her in for questioning. She told the police of her husband's movements and statements before leaving his home earlier that evening. She told police, "He left home about 5:30, saying he was going to Indianapolis." She continued, "As he left, he called back to one of our sons, Vinton Jr., and told him he would never see his father again as he was going to Indianapolis. I called to him because I knew he was angry with my family for not helping him to finance the mill in Indianapolis, and I told him if he went by my mother's home on his way to Indianapolis, to remember that he had two sons that had to bear his name and not to do anything that he would be ashamed of." She told police she didn't see him again that evening. Deborah continued, saying that her husband was not a drinking man and seldom, if ever, drank liquor. This was a strange comment, given that on October 31, 1918, her husband's name was among those listed in a nearly full-page advertisement in the *Cincinnati Enquirer* opposing Prohibition. "Unless it was worry over financial matters, I don't know what would have made him do it," she stated to police. He suffered a nervous breakdown two years earlier when he and his brother Lyman's grain business was dissolved. "Since then, he has worried a lot about his troubles," she continued. Deborah Perin told police that Vinton spent a lot of time in Indianapolis working on his mill. In a damning revelation, she also stated that she thought her husband had probably contemplated his actions before he left their home that evening.

According to reports, Deborah handled the tragedy with grace and resilience. She balanced concern for her sisters and her husband with fortitude. She was quick to say that she did not fear her husband and that he would never return to their home.

During the investigation, it was discovered that the late Mrs. Rawson had a broken wrist. At first, investigators surmised that Perin had grabbed her wrist during a struggle and twisted her arm, breaking her wrist. However, the Rawson sisters explained that their mother had broken her wrist in a fall some months earlier.

The next morning, police searched the Norwood home of Vinton and Deborah Perin. There, Detectives Bullerdick, Brink, and Hanrahan, along with Norwood detective Lee Kiley, found evidence supporting the theory of premeditation. At the home, they secured a box of cartridges and a bottle of gun cleaner. The gun cleaner had been opened, and some of the contents were missing, indicating that it had been used recently. Perin's sons told detectives that the cartridges had been purchased recently.

In the search for the missing suspect, police in Bellefontaine, Ohio, detained a man who matched Perin's description. He was later released when he proved that he was a Cincinnati businessman on his way to Detroit on a business trip. On September 29, three days after the shooting, Perin phoned Safety Director Charles E. Tudor and Detective Chief Emmett D. Kirgan and proposed his surrender by way of a meeting.

When Perin surrendered, his clothes were soaked, and he had three days of stubble on his face. Perin readily confessed to shooting his mother-in-law and sister-in-law. He stated that since he left the scene of the crime he had "just walked and walked" without direction or plan. Perin said that he had, without meaning to, headed south into Kentucky. He walked thirty-five miles from Cincinnati to Walton, Kentucky. He spent the night in Walton. The next day, he decided to return home, thinking that it would be best for his family. During his confession, Perin often paced the floor and wept. His recollection of that fateful evening's events differed slightly from those of Nina and the housekeeper. He confessed: "I did not mean to kill her and shoot her daughter. I only meant to scare them into giving me money to finance my flour mill in Indianapolis. I drew the revolver, intending to point it to the ceiling, and in my excitement, I pulled the trigger."

At police headquarters, Vinton Perin was searched. In his pockets, they found poison tablets. When asked about the tablets, Perin gave vague, elusive answers. One answer he gave was that he had had them for quite some time and had put them in his pocket so that they would be safe from his family accidentally taking them. Detective Chief Kirgan asked Perin if suicide had entered his mind before or since the shooting. Perin replied, "No, that would have been a cowardly thing to do." H.R. Rightmire, the court stenographer, captured Perin's every word.

During his police interview, Perin rambled on, making statements about how he felt persecuted by his mother-in-law. She had "annoyed" him over the twenty years they had known each other. Perin said he intended to go to Indiana the night of the shooting, but before he left Cincinnati, he wanted "to pull a bluff" and scare Fanny into giving him money to finance the mill "so I could tell the lawyers in Indianapolis something." He continued: "I always carry a revolver when I go to Indianapolis. It is pretty tough at the yards." Police continued to question Perin. He was remanded to the Hamilton County jail.

A week later, he was allowed to see his family and was visited by his wife and two sons. While his family was visiting him, Perin got word that a Hamilton County grand jury was bringing an indictment against him for first-degree murder in the death of Francis D. Rawson and a second indictment for shooting to kill and wound (today called attempted murder) his sister-in-law Nina Rawson. Deborah Perin made no statement confirming or denying whether she would give testimony against her husband. Vinton Perin stated that his wife and sons would stand by him during his trial.

Perin was arraigned before Judge Thomas H. Darby, and a trial date was set. His counsel, attorney James R. Clark, conferred with his client, who looked weak and tired. Perin was unable to speak due to bouts of weeping, so his attorney pled not guilty on his behalf. The plea was expected to be not guilty by reason of insanity.

Another twist in the case came when it was revealed through court documents that Francis D. Rawson left no will. Her daughter Deborah, wife of her accused killer, sued the estate for one-seventh of the total Rawson fortune, which included several properties around Hamilton County. While Deborah was filing paperwork over the estate of her late mother, her husband was being seated before Judge John A.C. Caldwell of the criminal division of common pleas court. It was noted that seventy-five citizens were on the venire as potential jurors; sixteen of those were women.

On November 10, the murder trial of Vinton Perin began. However, almost immediately, Judge Caldwell delayed the trial until November 28 at the request of the defense. He did insist that the impaneling of the jury continue.

The trial finally began on December 5, when Nina Rawson took the stand to be questioned by prosecuting attorney Charles Bell and the assistant prosecutor, Nelson Schwab. She gave testimony that reflected the events she had outlined during the investigation, this time under oath. She was dressed in a black dress appropriate for a lady of the era in mourning. Her arm was still in a sling, as she was recuperating from the gunshot wound inflicted by the accused, her brother-in-law. Her testimony was heart-wrenching. She sobbed through every detail of the murder of her mother. She mentioned that she "disliked" Perin and had for the past decade. Nina testified that she had given money to her sister Deborah to help her family situation. She further testified that she had given Vinton a small amount of money in the sum of $2,500 on July 24, 1923, to help with his grain operations, but that it was his demand for more money that set off the chain of events that led to the shooting of herself and her mother. Her testimony continued. She stated that she had given her sister funds for rent and other expenses after seeing that she was "desperately in need of money." Nina continued to testify for the jury about the dire financial situation of her sister, explaining some of the events prior to the shooting.

Josephine Rawson, the youngest daughter of the victim and witness to the alleged crimes, took the stand on December 8. She began her testimony by stating that she was in the next room behind a curtain when the shooting occurred but that she entered the library in time to see Vinton Perin standing with the revolver still in his hand. He demanded that she stop. She continued her testimony and relayed the rest of her knowledge of the events. Miss Schuelter, the housekeeper, testified next. Her testimony echoed her statements to the detectives during the investigation. Joseph Rawson was called as a witness, as were several others. At the conclusion of this testimony, the State of Ohio rested its case.

Deborah Perin was the primary witness for the defense. She gave her testimony as laid out in the investigation. However, she did reveal that she had been at times suicidal due to her family's financial situation. She testified that she considered taking poison, which lent validity to why her husband had taken poison tablets from the house and had them in his possession when he was taken into custody. Her sons also testified as to what they had seen and known. Vinton showed the most emotion in court when his family was on the stand, sometimes weeping profusely into his hands.

Since not guilty by reason of insanity was the plea, both the defense and the prosecution brought forth professional alienists (today known as psychiatrists) who had previously examined Vinton. Arguments were made both for and against the insanity defense. The defense labeled his actions over the previous years as "queer" (a word that, in those days, meant strange or odd, with no sexual connotation). Vinton's brother, Lyman, testified next. He swore on the stand that he thought his brother was insane ever since their fistfight a couple of years earlier, and he still considered him crazy. On cross-examination, Lyman admitted that he and his brother had reconciled. "I have only a brotherly interest, only to bring out that which is right, fair, and square. I have no other interest," the older brother testified.

The defense called May Perin Prather, Vinton's sister, to testify that her brother had changed in his mental functioning for the worse in the previous several years. Many other witnesses were brought down from Indianapolis, all testifying that in some way or another they knew that financial strains on Perin were causing mental and emotional deficits.

Vinton Perin did not take the stand in his own defense. The defense closed with the statements of two alienists, who both testified that Perin was insane. One of the alienists described him as "dull, apathetic, and indifferent to the whole situation." When asked to explain why the defense did not put Perin on the stand, his council, James Clark and Burton E. Robinson, said that their client was too unstable to take the stand. They declared that he would not be able to make it through testimony without breaking from reality completely. As it turned out, it was during the testimony of his wife that Perin broke down and wept uncontrollably. He was clearly emotional beyond his ability to contain it.

The trial concluded on December 11 and went to the jury for deliberation.

On Saturday morning, December 13, 1924, the *Cincinnati Enquirer* headline read, "Jury Acquits Vinton Perin; Insanity Verdict Surprise; Mental Test Is to Be Faced."

"Not guilty, upon the sole ground of insanity," was the verdict on the charge of first-degree murder. The judgment was rendered after just fifty-five minutes of deliberation. The jury took only two ballots.

When the verdict was read aloud, the spectators in the gallery gasped. They had been expecting a guilty verdict or at least a verdict of second-degree manslaughter. Perin slowly rose from his seat, looking as if he could use a good night's sleep. He seemed to be unaware of what was happening around him. According to witnesses, Perin turned to look for his wife, but she was not in the courtroom at that time. The judge calmed the courtroom, and Perin was led back to his cell at the Hamilton County jail; he was still facing an additional charge of attempted murder of his sister-in-law.

With the verdict on the books, Perin became the first person in the history of Hamilton County to be found not guilty by reason of insanity.

After some wrangling with attorneys and alienists, sentencing Judge William H. Lueders declared that the evidence had convinced him that Perin was insane. The judge reprimanded him to the State Hospital for the Criminally Insane in Lima, Ohio, for an unspecified time. Perin would not be released until he was deemed sane and no longer a threat to himself or society. Perin put up no legal impediments to his admission to the state hospital. His attorneys argued that he might have some course to reverse the probate court's insane designation, rendering him legally sane, but that would leave him eligible to be tried on the second indictment of attempted murder, with prejudice of sanity no longer an option.

Many who kept up with the case thought that Perin would serve only a short time in the asylum and would soon be released as sane. However, on arrival there, his mental condition deteriorated. If he was not unhinged before, he was soon after that.

In December 1925, one year after the trial and verdict in the Rawson murder case, Judge Stanley Struble distributed the estate of the late Mrs. Rawson, who had died without a will. Deborah Perin was the plaintiff in the partitioning of the estate. The home was sold for a total of $155,300. After taxes and fees, each of Francis Rawson's seven children received $20,833.20. An *Enquirer* article explaining this deliberation mentioned that Deborah left Cincinnati and moved to Miami, Florida. The article also indicated that her husband was still confined to the State Hospital for the Criminally Insane at Lima.

Court records from Miami indicate that Deborah and Vinton Perin were divorced in that city in 1929. Those records do not indicate whether Vinton was still incarcerated. However, a *Cincinnati Enquirer* article dated January 8, 1930, noted that Vinton Perin was still an inmate at the asylum in Lima. Remember, insanity would legally be considered a medical condition, and medical records are sealed. No trial was ever held for the attempted murder of Nina Rawson.

Vinton Perin lived out the remainder of his life in mental institutions, mostly at Lima. He outlived both his former wife and his eldest son, Warren.

Nina Rawson died in 1943. She was interred alongside her mother, father and three of her sisters in Spring Grove Cemetery.

Vinton Perin died in 1954 (some sources indicate 1949) at the age of eighty from arteriosclerosis. He was buried at Evergreen Cemetery in Southgate, Campbell County, Kentucky. From south of the river he came, and to it he returned.

The grave of Nina F. Rawson in Spring Grove Cemetery. In an odd twist, she was ultimately outlived by her would-be killer. *Photo by Nancy Heizer.*

One last twist in the Rawson family saga came on December 25, 1955. Nina Rawson, niece of Nina and Josephine and granddaughter of the late Francis D. Rawson, was involved in a strange incident while living at Hotel Sinton. A cousin in California mailed her a pipe bomb. The cousin, Edward Rawson Perin, was born Vinton Perin Jr., the son of Vinton and Deborah (née Rawson) Perin. He had changed his name on entering the U.S. Army. While the bomb proved to be a dud, it did contain a two-foot length of pipe with glass bottles of liquid and pieces of sharp metal. The odd and rambling letter that came with it boasted that it was "Power Unequalled." The note further claimed that it was the nephew's "Dearest Possession." A frightened Nina turned it over to Detective Faragher, and his examination concluded that it was harmless. No reason was ever discovered for its mailing. Historians are left to wonder if it had any connection to the family murder case of 1924.

AUTHOR'S NOTE: THE CRIME described here is, at its core, one of murder over money for a grain factory. Bread is made from grain, but it is also a slang term for money. Hence the chapter's title, "Bread or Bullets."

15

JAMES HOSKINS

MURDERING LUNATIC OR AGENDA-PUSHING MADMAN?

O n the morning of Wednesday, October 15, 1980, one of the strangest crimes in Cincinnati history unfolded at WCPO on Central Avenue and Fifth Street. At about 2:00 a.m., a man named James Hoskins, armed with five handguns, a semi-automatic rifle, and hundreds of rounds of ammunition, took over the WCPO newsroom. He had held Elaine Green and her cameraman at gunpoint in the parking lot and forced his way into the building, where he took seven more hostages. He seized the newsroom for the next twelve hours. He held a gun to Green and told her to interview him on camera. She agreed. Hoskins admitted to Green that he had killed his girlfriend, Melanie Finlay, before coming to the station. He told police where to find Finlay's body: in their apartment on Twelfth and Vine Streets in Over-the-Rhine.

"I blew my girlfriend away tonight. She's dead. I'm a dead man," he told Green. "There is no hope for me. I'm slipping away. I'm gone. I'm gone." He also said that he had "taken weird drugs," mentioning angel dust and valium. During the standoff, police went to Hoskins' apartment. After carefully entering to avoid any booby traps he may have set, they found a large cache of weapons and Melanie Finlay. Frank P. Cleveland, Hamilton County Coroner, pronounced Finlay dead from "multiple gunshot wounds to the head and chest." Finlay, an eighth-grade teacher at Assumption School in Mount Healthy, was just thirty-one years old. She was also a former nun, according to a 1980 Associated Press article. Hoskins and Finlay's apartment had extensive files on prominent city figures, labeled "political creeps,"

James Hoskins' apartment in Over-the-Rhine, which he shared with his girlfriend, Melanie Finlay. The apartment became her murder site prior to his taking hostages at WCPO. *Photo by Nancy Heizer.*

"business creeps" and "police tactics." Investigators said Hoskins was extremely focused on race and poverty, both subjects he mentioned during the bizarre interview with Green. Police found equipment and materials for bombs and more weapons at the Twelfth Street apartment. Al Schottelkotte, a local newscaster, joined police on their initial search of the apartment when Finlay's body was discovered. Hoskins, a former U.S. Marine who still had a bullet in his hip from his time in the service, said he and Finlay had planned the station takeover. He said: "This whole thing was planned back in San Francisco. I can't say if it was the drugs...we had planned to do this together, and I went berserk. She's dead."

That morning, viewers in Cincinnati turned on their televisions to see evening anchor Al Schottelkotte reporting live from the newsroom parking lot.

Hoskins held nine WCPO employees hostage. During the twelve-hour standoff, he rambled about several things. "We never did arrive at his true motivation," said Lieutenant Dale Menkhaus, who attempted to negotiate with Hoskins during the siege. "He talked about many things, about being a revolutionary. He wanted to make changes to society." Hoskins spoke repeatedly about the plight of the poor. He made all kinds of accusations against the press, the police and society at large. "He was the coldest human I've ever encountered," Menkhaus said. "I tried to carefully say, 'Well, you know, we're not sure of her condition,' and he was very clear. He said, 'She's dead. I made sure she was dead.' He was pretty cold." Hoskins kept his weapon trained on the hostages while Green's photographer kept the camera trained on Hoskins. Green interviewed him to get his story and to keep him distracted. While Hoskins never did seem to get to any identifiable point, his rambling led some to think he might have been mentally disturbed. He was, according to the hostages, mostly unintelligible. He clearly wanted attention, and he got it.

Hoskins eventually let his hostages go. He then shot and killed himself while on the phone with Menkhaus. "When he finally actually did it, he told me, 'Well, it's time. I'm going to do it now,'" Menkhaus said. "In a monotone voice, no emotion, he simply said, 'I'm going to do it,' and I heard the gunshot. That was as cold as anything I've ever been part of." After more investigation, Menkhaus said he classified Hoskins as "a terrorist whose goal was to promote anarchy." Coroner Cleveland said Hoskins died of a single gunshot wound to the head from a .38 revolver. In addition, Hoskins had a .22 hidden in his hat when the coroner investigated the corpse.

James Hoskin's siege on WCPO was broadcast in part as it unfolded. All around greater Cincinnati, people watched with great enthusiasm the scene play out. They sat enraptured as Hoskins waved his gun and proselytized. Al Schottelkotte reported it all. It was one of the most-watched local broadcasts of the 1980s.

Initially, Cincinnati police said they would "never know" why Hoskins did what he did. During an interview, Hoskins' mother, Pearl, stated to the police that she did not know why he would take the life of his girlfriend, hold hostages at the television station and ultimately commit suicide. She was quoted as saying: "It was a complete shock to me. I have no idea why. He has suffered from spells of depression, but he was down here last night between 8:00 and 8:30 and returned some money he had borrowed. He was in a good mood; he was laughing." The investigation shed some light on Hoskins' past and, therefore, his motivations. He was known among his friends as "a nice guy" and "a dedicated artist." He was into fitness and was an avid bodybuilder. Hoskins was a black belt in karate, a discipline he took seriously. He also collected and studied antiques and foreign weapons. One friend who was interviewed stated that Hoskins collected weapons, but did so for historical study, not stockpiling for a future event.

The reactions to the tragedy resounded in articles written in the days after the events. Some folks thought well of Hoskins' motivation of raising awareness about the plight of the underprivileged. In contrast, others wrote him off as a terrorist and a murderer. A *Cincinnati Enquirer* writer penned a cold, ruthless and judgmental article portraying Hoskins as a condescending hypocrite for not donating to poverty programs. Other writers showed a more nuanced approach to Hoskins and his actions, speculating that he may have had an undiagnosed mental illness, or that desperation drove him to extremes. As a romantic side note, reporters Al Schottelkotte and Elaine Green were married not long after the incident. Green had become something of a local hero for her courage in the face of danger. She would go on to win a Peabody Award for her interview with Hoskins. Whatever the case, James Hoskins' crimes have become the stuff of urban folk tales in Cincinnati.

16
THE INFLUENZA PANDEMIC OF 1918-1919

In 1918–19, an influenza outbreak swept across a large swath of America, including Cincinnati and the surrounding area. It was sometimes called the "Spanish flu," an odd name given that its origins have never been determined conclusively. It started in Boston in America. The outbreak made thousands of Ohioans and Kentuckians sick and cost hundreds of them their lives.

Schools were shut down and the empty buildings used as temporary makeshift hospitals. What had been classrooms became patient wards. In those days, ammonia was a regular cleaning agent, and soon the streets began to smell of death and disinfectant. The old schoolhouse in Clifton was one such converted facility. Residents there still claim you can get a whiff of ammonia when you walk down the halls. The outbreak brought Cincinnati to a standstill.

The influenza outbreak of 1919 was the worst such incident in American history. It went on for more than a year. In total, it killed around 50 million people worldwide (when the world's total population was much smaller than today) and 675,000 Americans. It affected 25 to 35 percent of the population. There had been previous influenza outbreaks in America, including one in 1889–90. However, in prior outbreaks, it was generally infants, the elderly, those with an underlying condition or compromised immune systems who were most vulnerable. During the 1919 epidemic, it was overwhelmingly healthy people between the ages of eighteen and sixty who were affected. Symptoms ranged from typical flu conditions—aches, pains,

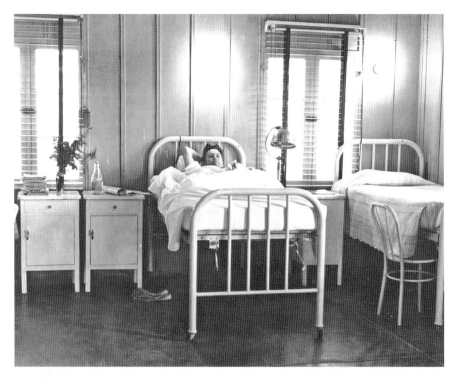

A patient recuperating from the Spanish flu. *Photo in public domain.*

fever, headache, congestion, and vomiting—to more detrimental symptoms, such as hemorrhaging from orifices. Lungs would often fill with fluid, slowly drowning the infected person. Some people died directly from the influenza within a few days of contracting it. Others died from secondary causes like dehydration and pneumonia. The 1918–19 pandemic was different than any other the world had seen, because it came in three distinct waves. Previous outbreaks were characterized by one wave with limited dispersion and only affected one geographic area.

Scientists believe the difference was due to an explosion in the world's population—the more people, the more rapid the spread. The 1918–19 pandemic claimed an estimated fifty million lives, among them approximately half a million American lives. In America, the first wave appeared in the spring of 1918 but dissipated over the summer. It returned in the fall and continued into winter. The third wave came in the early winter of 1919 and lasted for well over four months. Of the three waves, the second was the most catastrophic. As is the case today, many theories abounded. One theory at the time claimed that it began in Spain in the spring of 1918, as evidenced by the large number of people documented as infected there, hence the name "Spanish flu." In 1918, America was engulfed in the Great War (later called World War I). It was thought that servicemen coming home may have brought it to America.

Much like the recent COVID-19 pandemic, the influenza pandemic was fought by prohibiting crowds, wearing medical masks, and shutting down businesses and public gatherings in spaces such as parks and beaches. Citizens were encouraged to stop spitting and coughing in public. Some citizens tried alternative treatments that ranged from sacrificing animals to putting clothes clips on their noses. The Rosenow vaccine was tried but was later proved to be ineffective. Women who were pregnant were more likely to have complications. Among those women who survived, many lost their babies to the infection. The economy also took a dramatic hit, with the closure of all kinds of businesses and services. It was the dawn of the Roaring Twenties, and Prohibition had not yet been implemented. While other businesses suffered, the liquor industry thrived. Then, as suddenly as it had appeared in 1918, the disease seemed to disappear. Cases dropped off quickly, and the disease seemed to have run its course. While the pandemic itself was over, its consequences continued for years afterward.

The worldwide loss of life was estimated at over 50 million, while the number of deaths in America was estimated at more than 675,000. Spring Grove Cemetery, as well as other cemeteries in greater Cincinnati, dedicated whole sections to the victims of the 1918–19 pandemic. The economy took years to rebuild. Nearly an entire generation of young people was lost. As a result of the influenza pandemic, the average life expectancy in Cincinnati dropped by twelve years. Although a relatively effective vaccine was developed in 1945 and sanitation standards were much improved, a second influenza outbreak happened in America in 1957 and 1958. It took a toll of 70,000 lives.

17
THE CHOLERA OUTBREAK

In the mid-1800s, a cholera outbreak in Cincinnati killed hundreds of people, and many more were left extremely sick. While medicine then was not as advanced as it is today, doctors knew that cholera was primarily caused by stagnant water that had become infected. Cholera caused extreme stomach discomfort, and intestinal inflammation, as well as severe diarrhea, vomiting, dehydration, fatigue, and weakness. It would throw off a person's electrolyte balance and even cause low blood pressure and a rapid heart rate. There was no effective treatment for cholera in those days. Some doctors tried a chemical solution called calomel. However, in many patients, calomel, which contained mercury, made them even sicker. A large number of patients actually died from mercury poisoning.

At the time, most Cincinnatians lived in what was called the "Basin," a mostly flat semicircle that encompassed most of what we know today as downtown. The Miami and Erie Canal, a waterway that ran from Toledo through downtown to the Ohio River, was also responsible for dramatically perpetuating the outbreak. While the Miami and Erie Canal was a waterway used for the transportation of goods through the Midwest, it was extremely unsanitary. Cattle were used to drag barges along it by pulling the goods from a towpath. Cattle dung was swept into the canal. Chamber pots were routinely dumped into it as well. People swam in the canal (and inevitably urinated in it as well). The water stood stagnant in places. The Miami and Erie Canal was filthy, it stank, and it was a breeding ground for diseases like cholera. It ran through the Over-the-Rhine neighborhood behind what was

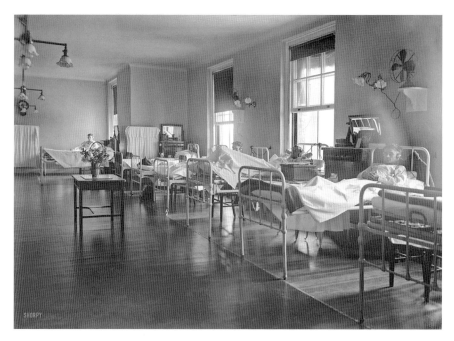

A patient ward in a makeshift hospital during the cholera outbreak of the mid-1800s. *Courtesy of Pinterest.*

then the city's insane asylum. In those years, the asylum was on the outskirts of Cincinnati proper and was some yards from the nearest house. The asylum used the canal as its primary source of water. It was later speculated that the unsanitary water from the canal perpetuated illnesses, both mental and physical, at the asylum. Over time, the inmates experienced all manner of stomach aches and intestinal issues. Sanitation practices were not what they are today, and the whole asylum must have had a wretched stench. Modern medicine equates clean water with good hygiene and good hygiene with good mental health.

In the 1700s and 1800s, death was an up-close part of daily life. Many children died in infancy and early childhood. Many parents died of various diseases as well, leaving cities such as Cincinnati with a large number of orphans. Children and infants who, in many cases, didn't have other relatives to stay with were sent to the city-run orphanage, where nothing but their most basic needs were met. The area beside the asylum, ground that was later used for the construction of the Cincinnati Music Hall, was where the city's orphanage was located. For several years, doctors couldn't understand why the children at the orphanage were getting sick and dying in such large numbers. Health officials eventually determined that the orphans' ongoing illnesses were due to contaminated water from the Miami and Erie Canal.

Many of the adults who died at the asylum and children who died at the orphanage were buried in an uncharted graveyard beside the asylum, a cemetery for unclaimed corpses known as a "potter's field." When the cholera outbreak was finally under control, both the asylum and the orphanage were moved farther out of town. The old facilities were torn down. Some of the bodies were reinterred at Spring Grove Cemetery for proper burial. However, many of the unmarked graves remained undisturbed. A few years later, in 1878, Cincinnati Music Hall (and, after that, the Hamilton County Memorial Hall) was built on the site of the former asylum and orphanage and potter's field graveyard. Due to its history, many folks say that the Cincinnati Music Hall is haunted by the ghosts of the unknown children buried within its grounds.

Cincinnati has always had a large Jewish population, and the earliest congregations needed a burial ground. Seeing this need, Morris Moses and Joseph Jonas purchased land from Nicholas Longworth, a prominent socialite, for seventy-five dollars. The Chestnut Street Cemetery was opened in 1821 in the West End neighborhood, now known as the Betts-Longworth Historic District. As the cholera epidemic spread across Cincinnati, the cemetery filled up rather quickly. It was closed in 1849 because of the epidemic and had a total of eighty-five burials.

A total of eight thousand Cincinnatians died during the cholera epidemic of 1849. Among those lost was the infant son of the famous author Harriet Beecher Stowe. The Ohio State Fair was postponed in 1850, as was the Constitutional Convention of 1851 and 1852.

As a result of the epidemic, many sought to move out of the filth of the basin and farther up into the hills surrounding Cincinnati. However, the steep hills proved to be a challenge for developers and those wishing to escape the muck. Roads into the hills were insufficient. Some residents were able to build on the newly renamed Mount Adams. Many residents fled to Mount Pleasant, up a wagon trail about ten miles north of the city.

They took refuge in the elevated community that offered fresh air and (because of its elevated geography) fresh water that was not stagnant. Soon, Mount Pleasant became the place to go for well-to-do residents of Cincinnati. The town grew rapidly.

In a few short years, Mount Pleasant capitalized on its new healthy status and renamed itself Mount Healthy. Schools were built, and a train

The Chestnut Street Cemetery, a Jewish burial ground that was filled up during the cholera outbreak of 1849. *Photo by Roy Heizer.*

depot was established. It became an active and charming small town on the outskirts of Cincinnati.

Although records are obscure, local legend says that the trains that used to run from Cincinnati were not allowed to stop in Mount Healthy during the influenza epidemic of 1919, because the people in Mount Healthy were afraid of contamination. Soon, town officials removed the train depot altogether in an attempt to avoid more illnesses reaching its residences. Today, citizens say one can hear the whistle of the train when you are standing in the streets at the pinnacle of Mount Healthy—the whistle of a ghost train carrying the dead from below the hills.

While there is no train through Mount Healthy now, if one listens carefully on a calm, quiet evening, one might be able to hear the trains in Northside… or is it something else?

18

THE GRAVE ROBBERY OF JOHN SCOTT HARRISON

John Scott Harrison was born on October 4, 1804, in Vincennes, Indiana. He was the son of U.S. president William Henry Harrison and First Lady Anna Harrison and the grandson of Declaration of Independence signer Benjamin Harrison V. In 1852, he graduated from Miami University in Oxford, Ohio, just north of Cincinnati. That fall, he was elected to the U.S. House of Representatives as a member of the Whig Party. He was reelected in 1854 as an Opposition Party member, serving from 1854 to 1857. In 1857, he was defeated and returned to his estate, Point Farm, in North Bend, about fifteen miles west of Cincinnati on the Ohio River. His first marriage, to Lucretia Knapp Johnson, produced three children. After she left him a widower, he married Elizabeth Ramsey Irwin. That marriage produced ten children, including Benjamin Harrison, who would become the twenty-third president of the United States. This makes John Scott Harrison the only man in American history to have been both the son and the father of a U.S. president. Another interesting fact is that his body was stolen from its grave and sold to the Ohio Medical College for dissection, igniting a national scandal.

John Scott Harrison died in his sleep on the night of May 25, 1878. Funeral services were held at the Presbyterian church in Cleves, just west of Cincinnati proper. Many family and friends attended the funeral, including his son Benjamin. Harrison's mortal remains were laid to rest at the family plot in Congress Green Cemetery in North Bend, Ohio, on May 29. During his funeral procession, attendees noticed that the nearby grave

A portrait of John
Scott Harrison.
*Original illustration by
Alison Limbach Pfeifer.*

of a family member, Augustus Devin, who had died eleven days earlier of tuberculosis, had been robbed.

In the eighteenth and nineteenth centuries, grave robbing was a big business. Many graves were raided for jewelry or other possessions, while some were robbed for the body itself. In those days, medical schools would pay good money for fresh corpses on which to perform dissections and experiments.

This robbery was cause for great alarm among the Harrison family, and sons Benjamin, Carter, and John saw to it that their father's grave was secured. The metal casket was laid in a deep brick vault, and the grave was reinforced with large stone slabs over the casket. All the bricks were then covered with cement. After the cement had dried, the grave was backfilled. The Harrisons went so far as to pay a watchman thirty dollars to guard the grave for thirty nights. The watchman was to either stay at the grave or make hourly rounds to oversee the security of the grave.

The next day, June 6, John Harrison and his cousin George Eaton obtained a warrant to search the Ohio Medical College for the body of their relative

Augustus Devin. They were assisted by a Constable Lacey and a detective named Snelbaker. Also in attendance were three Cincinnati police officers.

In the mid-1800s, medical schools were prime suspects in grave-robbing cases; they were notorious for stocking their anatomy classes with cadavers sold to them by "resurrection men." The *Cincinnati Enquirer* reported that suspicious activity had occurred overnight and that things were being moved in the alley near the Ohio Medical College. The general impression stated in the *Enquirer* was that a "stiff" was being smuggled into the Ohio Medical College.

The search party was met at the medical college entrance by a janitor, a man named Marshall. He escorted them while they searched the building. In the cellar, they found a chute connected to a door in the alley, which also connected to a dark vertical shaft running the height of the brick building. Elsewhere on the premises, they encountered crates of assorted human body parts and a student doing research on the corpse of a woman. They also found the body of a six-month-old baby, but no Augustus Devin.

Finally, Marshall insisted that he needed to go and alert the faculty as to the search. Detective Snelbaker let him go but put a junior deputy on his trail. Marshall didn't get a member of the faculty; instead, he went to the upper floors of the facility. Marshall unknowingly led the deputy to an upstairs room with a windlass (a type of hand-cranked winch) and a rope running into a square hole in the floor. That hole led into the long, dark shaft they had seen in the basement. The windlass was used to lift cadavers to the upper rooms of the building.

Snelbaker noticed that the rope was taut. He turned the windlass crank and slowly drew up a corpse from inside the shaft. The cadaver was naked except for a cloth wrapped around its head. John Harrison dismissed this corpse at first. The body was that of a relatively robust man, not the emaciated twenty-three-year-old body of consumption victim Devin that they were looking for. Detective Snelbaker suggested that he check the identity of the corpse nonetheless, so Harrison unwrapped the cloth from around the man's head.

Harrison's face became white as a ghost as the blood drained from his features. "It's father," he gasped. John Scott Harrison, whose burial his sons had attended less than twenty-four hours before, had been dumped down a dank chute in the dead of night. One can imagine the horror and anger that the young John Harrison experienced on discovering his father's body in such a state. Devin's body was later discovered in the pickling vats at the University of Michigan. John Harrison immediately hired the Cincinnati undertaking firm Estep & Meyer, located at 214 West Seventh Street, to care for his father's body until he could consult with other family members and arrangements could be made to handle the now displaced body. The body was briefly interred in a temporary vault at Spring Grove Cemetery in Cincinnati. Sometime later, it was reinterred securely in the vault of his father, President William Henry Harrison, at North Bend, down the road from Congress Green Cemetery.

An inspection was made of the grave to ascertain precisely how the robbers could have obtained the corpse from a secured site. The stones at the foot of the coffin were ajar, and the coffin had been drilled into along its side. The lid had been pried up so the corpse could be roped by the feet and pulled out. It was believed that the thieves must have seen the measures taken at the Harrison burial, or they would have tried for the head and been foiled by the much larger and heavier stones and cement covering the other end. The watchman had no explanation as to how robbers could have stolen the corpse. The Harrisons suspected that the watchman was in on it, but they had no evidence; therefore, no charges were filed against him.

George Eaton's brother Archie and Carter Harrison stayed in Cincinnati to tell their families what had happened. Carter told John that their father's body had been stolen; John told Carter that he already knew, because he had found it at the medical college. They had the janitor arrested for receiving and concealing the unlawfully removed body of their revered father. The medical college faculty posted the $5,000 bond, and Marshall was quickly released.

John Scott Harrison's final resting place in the family crypt. *Courtesy of Necro Tourist TNT Images (c) 2014. Photo: Ken Naegele, www.necrotourist.com.*

116

The Ohio Medical College was accused of fraud and ethics violations in the newspapers, but the faculty was overwhelmingly obtuse. They were sorry that such a revered man as John Scott Harrison had been found in their dissection rooms, but that was the cost of modern medical education. During the investigation, as the scandal swirled, Carter Harrison decided to visit the Ohio Medical College to examine the location where his father's body had been discovered. History recounts that while he was at the college, he encountered one Dr. W. Seely, the secretary of the school as well as one of the professors. It was a horribly unfortunate meeting. The doctor, who was already enraged by the newspaper criticism leveled at the college and the faculty, indelicately remarked to the grief-stricken Carter Harrison that the entire affair didn't matter, since it would all be the same for everyone on the day of resurrection. Neither history nor the Harrisons would forget or forgive that callous remark.

On June 11, Dr. Robert Bartholow, dean of the college, published a statement in the *Cincinnati Times* denying knowledge of the theft or responsibility for an anonymous resurrectionist taking "this means to replenish his exchequer [coffers]." The statement seemed disingenuous at best.

That afternoon, Harrison published his anguished and furious rebuttal in an open letter.

> *Your janitor denied that it lay upon your tables, but the clean incision into the carotid artery, the tread with which it was ligatured, the injected veins, prove him a liar. Who made that incision and injected that body, gentlemen of the faculty? The surgeons that examined the body say that it was no bungler. While he lay upon your table, the long white beard, which hands of infant grandchildren had often stroked in love, was rudely shorn from his face. Have you so little care of your college that an unseen and an unknown man may do all this? Who took him from that table and hung him by the neck in the pit?*

On June 16, 1878, the body of Augustus Devin arrived in Cincinnati to a group of 150 Harrison family members and citizens. Young Devin's remains were, for a second time, interred in a grave. This time, though, it would be watched and guarded day and night. The grave of Devin was never disturbed again.

With no indictments against or answers from the Ohio Medical College faculty forthcoming, Benjamin Harrison filed a civil suit. The criminal and civil suits' outcomes are lost to history, as all records were destroyed

An illustration of a grave robbery, late 1800s. *Original illustration by Alison Limbach Pfeifer.*

when the Hamilton County Courthouse burned down during the riots of 1884—a tragedy of historic proportions.

In reaction to the Harrison horror, Ohio, Indiana, Illinois, Iowa, and Michigan passed amended Anatomy Acts that increased penalties for grave robbing and allowed medical schools to use only unclaimed bodies of people who died in the care of the state (paupers, orphans, the insane, prisoners) for anatomical dissection. But enforcement was lax. Demand far exceeded supply. As a result, "resurrection men" would continue to practice their morose but lucrative trade well into the twentieth century.

As A WICKED SIDE note: As a direct result of the Harrison Grave robbery, a Cincinnati-based inventor named Andrew Van Bibber created what he called the "Mort-Safe" in 1878. He went on to patent the device. After Van Bibber's "Mort-Safe" invention, George W. Boyd of Springfield, Ohio, patented the first metal grave vault to use the air bell principle in 1879.

The purpose of both devices was to stop grave robbers from obtaining access to buried corpses. The devices worked exceptionally well, as they were both nearly impossible to break into. These were the first two attempts at creating the modern burial vault as we know it. Today, the burial vault is thought of as a means of protecting the body of a loved one from the elements of nature, but it was originally invented as a means of protecting the body of a loved one from the elements of criminal undertakings.

BIBLIOGRAPHY

Chapter 1. The Easter Sunday Slaughter

Cincinnati Enquirer. "Bereaved Cry for Murdered Kin." April 4, 1975.
————. "Butler Country Grand Jury Will Receive Hamilton's Eleven Victim Easter Murder Case." April 2, 1975.
————. "Easter Massacre Poses Puzzles." April 1, 1975.
————. "Eleven Persons Shot, Killed on Hamilton Southside." March 31, 1975.
————. "Funeral Rites Set Thursday for Slay Victims." April 2, 1975.
————. "Hamilton Slain Testimony Today." April 3, 1975.
————. "Jury Indicts Ruppert in Eleven Easter Killings." April 5, 1975.
————. "Jury Reports Today on Killings." April 4, 1975.
————. "Killer Sentenced." July 15, 1975.
————. "Metro." April 5, 1975.
————. "Ruppert Able to Stand Trial." May 13, 1975.
————. "Ruppert Condemned to Death in Dream." June 26, 1975.
————. "Ruppert Enters Prison." July 24, 1975.
————. "Ruppert Faces Judges." July 14, 1975.
————. "Ruppert Family Funeral Today at Sacred Heart." April 3, 1975.
————. "Ruppert Fearing Conspiracy, Slays Eleven in Rage: Psychiatrist." June 21, 1975.
————. "Ruppert Sanity Hearing Scheduled for May 12." April 10, 1975.
————. "Ruppert Trial Nearing Close; Three Judges May Rule Today." July 3, 1975.
————. "Sanity Exams Ordered." June 5, 1975.
————. "Slayings Suspect to Be Arraigned." April 8, 1975.
————. "While Eleven Are Buried, Suspect Is Indicted." April 5, 1975.

Chapter 2. Piatt Park and Its Sinister History

Cincinnati Enquirer archives. 1980.

Chapter 3. Lafcadio Hearn and the Tanyard Murder Case

Cincinnati Enquirer. "The Cases of Rufer and Egner." June 16, 1875.
————. "Coroner Maley Denies the Soft Impeachment." February 10, 1875.
————. "Details in Tanyard Murder." November 11, 1874.
————. "Details of Schilling Murder." May 27, 1875.
————. "The Furnace Fiends." November 13, 1874.
————. "The Furnace Fiends." November 14, 1874.
————. "The German Press." November 14, 1874.
————. "Herman Schilling Murder." February 5, 1875.
————. "Killed and Cremated." November 10, 1874.
————. "The Law Courts." March 12, 1875.
————. "No Relation." November 17, 1874.
————. "Over the Rhine." July 19, 1876.
————. "A Peep into the Jail." September 10, 1876.
————. "Rufer and Egner." July 1, 1875.
————. "The Rufer Trial." February 6, 1875.
————. "The Rufer Trial, the Charge of Judge Murdock." February 12, 1875.
————. "The Schilling Murder." January 29, 1875.
————. "The Schilling Murder." February 11, 1875.
————. "The Schilling Murder." April 23, 1875.
————. "The Schilling Murder, Preliminary Proceedings in the Trial of George Rufer." January 29, 1875.
————. "The Tannery Horror." November 12, 1874.
————. "The Tan-yard Horror." February 3, 1875.
————. "The Terrible Tannery Tragedy." November 11, 1874.
————. "Trial Notes." November 10, 1876.
————. "Violent Cremation." November 9, 1874.
McWilliams, Vera. *Lafcadio Hearn.* Boston, MA: Houghton Mifflin, 1946.
Murder by Gaslight. "The Tanyard Murder." www.murderbygaslight.com.
Paris Review. "The Many Lives of Lafcadio Hearn." https://www.theparisreview.org.
Public Library of Cincinnati and Hamilton County. Lafcadio Hearn Collection. https://www.cincinnatilibrary.org.

Chapter 4. Courthouse Riots of 1884

Cincinnati Enquirer. "Berner Sentence." March 29, 1884.
————. "100th Anniversary of Fire, Riot." March 4, 1984.

————. "William Berner Is Granted a Parole." June 5, 1895.

Rolfes, Steven J. *The Cincinnati Courthouse Riot*. New Orleans, LA: Pelican Publishing, 2016.

Chapter 5. Avondale Riots of 1967 and 1968

Cincinnati Enquirer. "Curfew Violations." April 17, 1968.

————. "For Most—Life Goes on as Usual in Tense Avondale." June 15, 1967.

————. "Guard Moves on Rioters; Curfew Slapped on City." April 9, 1968.

————. "Jury Gets Riot Case Today." August 2, 1968.

————. "Lt. Faces Hearing." August 1, 1967.

————. "Man 20 Convicted in Riot Night Case." September 20, 1967.

————. "Pride & Peace Go Up in Smoke of Hate." April 9, 1968.

Chapter 6. The Strangest Room in the House

Clara Barton Museum. "Death, Immortalized: Victorian Post-Mortem Photography." https://www.clarabartonmuseum.org.

Public Records. https://www.publicrecords.site/death-b.php?subid=prsrvc-broad-death-funerals.

Chapter 7. The Rhinock Report

Find a Grave. "Joseph Lafayette Rhinock." https://www.findagrave.com.

Wikipedia. "Joseph L. Rhinock." https://www.en.wikipedia.org.

————. "Robert W. Criswell." https://www.en.wikipedia.org.

Chapter 8. The Strange Story of Herbert S. Bigelow

Biographical Directory of the US Congress. "Bigelow, Herbert Seely." https://bioguideretro.congress.gov.

Ohio History Central. "Herbert S Bigelow." https://www.ohiohistorycentral.org.

Chapter 9. George "Boss" Cox: City Bosses and the Silent Grip on Power

Cincinnati Enquirer. "Ohio's Oil." January 10, 1890.

————. "Political Gossip." January 1, 1915.

————. "Receiver." January 15, 1915.

————. "Selections of One George B. Cox." September 25, 1895.

Koch, Herbert F. *An Ohio Warwick: Something of the Life & Times of George Barnsdale Cox*. Cincinnati, OH: 1916.

Chapter 10. Tragedy at the Avery House

Davies, Owen. *America Bewitched: The Story of Witchcraft after Salem*. Oxford, UK: Oxford University Press, 2013.
Find a Grave. "Coleman W. Avery." https://www.findagrave.com.
Geni. "Coleman W. Avery." https://www.geni.com.
Wikipedia. "Coleman W. Avery." https://wwww.en.wikipedia.org.

Chapter 11. Libby Holman, Actress or Murderess?

Cincinnati Enquirer. "Clean Slate Is Given to Libby." July 8, 1932.
———. "Libby and Son Off for Wilds of Africa." June 25, 1948.
———. "Libby Disappeared?" July 25, 1932.
———. "Libby Holman." April 25, 1937.
———. "Libby Holman Is Held as Material Witness." July 10, 1932.
———. "Libby Holman Released; Bond of $25,000 Posted." August 9, 1932.
———. "Libby Homan's Mate Is Victim of Bullet." July 7, 1932.
———. "Libby, in Seclusion, Eager for Trial Father Asserts." August 5, 1932.
———. "Mind a Blank, Libby Tells Jury." July 9, 1932.
———. "Sisters." December 18, 1932.
———. "Speculation over Fortune Revived." July 13, 1932.
———. "That Libby Reynolds Is Not at Cincinnati." July 24, 1932.

Chapter 12. Anna Marie Hahn

Cincinnati Enquirer. "Aged Mother Unaware." August 22, 1937.
———. "Aged Woman's Death Is Added to List in Hahn Investigation." August 20, 1937.
———. "Anna Hahn Is Confronted by 'Only Living Victim.'" October 27, 1937.
———. "Anna Hahn Is to Die for Murder Condemned by Jury." November 7, 1937.
———. "Anna Hahn Is to Die Tonight." December 7, 1938.
———. "Anna Hahn on Stand." November 1, 1937.
———. "Anna Hahn's Trial Halted Temporarily over Question of Embalming Powder." October 21, 1937.
———. "Arraignment Set for Today; Mrs. Hahn to Hear Charges." August 21, 1937.
———. "Arsenic." August 18, 1937.

———. "Blond Faces Renewal of State Quiz Today." November 3, 1937.
———. "Blond Is Linked with Another Poisoning; Indicted on Charges of Murdering Two." August 17, 1937.
———. "Court Dismisses Complaint of Anna Hahn's Attorneys; No Proof of Hampering." August 24, 1937.
———. "Courthouse Corridors Jammed." October 19, 1937.
———. "Defense Waits on Ruling." November 16, 1937.
———. "Expert Faces Final Quiz." October 29, 1937.
———. "Grave Opened; Poison Found in Palmer's Body, Is Claim of Surprise in Hahn Trial." October 25, 1937.
———. "Hahn Case." December 17, 1937.
———. "Hahn Counsel." September 22, 1937.
———. "Hahn Defense Wins First Point." October 5, 1937.
———. "Hahn Jurors at First Dinner Together." October 15, 1937.
———. "Hahn Jury Completed." October 15, 1937.
———. "Hahn Trial." October 13, 1937.
———. "Interview Is Off, Then Mrs. Hahn Relents." August 18, 1937.
———. "Isn't There Anybody Who Will 'Help Me.'" December 8, 1938.
———. "Poison Absent." September 9, 1937.
———. "Plan Dropped for Change of Venue." October 9, 1937.
———. "Property Willed to Children by Obendoerfer." September 10, 1937.
———. "Report of Chemist Attacked." September 27, 1937.
———. "To Escape 'Chair' Anna Hahn's Belief." November 25, 1937.
———. "Two Points Up for Decision Before Court Today in Anna Hahn Case." August 27, 1937.
———. "With 'Love and Kisses.'" August 19, 1937.
———. "Writing not Anna Hahn's." September 1, 1937.
Sawyer, Susan. *Speaking Ill of the Dead: Jerks in Ohio History*. Guilford, CT: Globe Pequot, 2016.

Chapter 13. The Ohio River Flood of 1937

Flood List. "The Ohio River Flood 1937." https://www.floodlist.com.
Ohio History Connection. "Ohio River Flood of 1937." https://www.ohiohistorycentral.org.
WCPO. "From the Vault." https://www.wcpo.com.

Chapter 14. Bread or Bullets: The Rawson Murder Case

Cincinnati Enquirer. "Bluff Ended in Shooting." September 30, 1924.
———. "Disappearance of Slayer Is Baffling." September 29, 1924.
———. "Early Trial of Perin Is Expected." October 1, 1924.
———. "Emotion Shown by Slayer." December 10, 1924.

———. "Jury Acquits Vinton Perin Insanity Verdict Surprise." December 13, 1924.

———. "Perin Declared to be Insane by Decree of Probate Court." December 24, 1924.

———. "Pleads Not Guilty." October 5, 1924.

———. "Police Net Is Evaded by Widow's Slayer." September 28, 1924.

———. "Rawson Estate Settled." December 13, 1925.

———. "Removed to Hospital." December 31, 1924.

———. "Rich Widow Is Slain in Home." September 27, 1924.

———. "Seeks Share in Estate." October 18, 1924.

———. "Slayer Fails to Take Stand." December 11, 1924.

———. "Slayer Sane, Alienist Testify." December 12, 1924.

———. "Testimony." December 6, 1924.

———. "Trial of Perin Is Continued." November 11, 1924.

———. "Trial to Be Resumed in Rawson Murder Case." November 27, 1924.

Townsend, J.T. *Queen City Notorious*. College Station, TX: Virtual Bookworm Publishing, 2014.

Chapter 15. James Hoskins: Murdering Lunatic or Agenda-Pushing Madman?

Cincinnati Enquirer. "Friends Aghast at Hoskins Violent End." October 16, 1980.

———. "Gun Shoots Killed Melanie Finley." Corner Reports, October 17, 1980.

———. "Hoskins Mother Regrets She Didn't Talk to Son." October 16, 1980.

———. "Terrified Hostages Feared for Lives." October 16, 1980.

———. "Top Local News Stories." December 28, 1980.

WCPO9. "From the Vault: The Day James Hoskins Held WCPO Newsroom Employees Hostage." https://www.wcpo.com.

Chapter 16. The Influenza Pandemic of 1918–1919

History. "Spanish Flu." https://www.history.com.

University of Cincinnati. "The 1918–19 Spanish Flu." https://digital.libraries.uc.edu.

WCPO. "1918 Flu: How Cincinnati Dealt with Modern History's Most Severe Pandemic." https://www.WCPO.com.

Chapter 17. The Cholera Outbreak

Centers for Disease Control and Prevention. "Cholera-Vibriocholerae Infection." https://www.cdc.gov.
Ohio History Central. "Cholera Epidemics." https://www.ohiohistorycentral.org.
University of Cincinnati Library. "The Irish in Cincinnati." https://.ed.edu.

Chapter 18. The Grave Robbery of John Scott Harrison

Cincinnati Enquirer. "The College Horror." June 4, 1878.
————. "The Grave Robbery, June 18, 1878.
————. "Honorable John Scott Harrison Torn from His Grave." May 31, 1878.
————. "Horror on Horror." June 13, 1878.
————. "Indianapolis Items." May 27, 1878.
————. "Practical Anatomy, The Harrison Horror." June 7, 1878.
Indiana Funeral Directors Association. "The Harrison Horror." https://www.infda.org.
Mental Floss. "The Body-Snatching Horror of John Scott Harrison." https://www.mentalfloss.com.

ABOUT THE AUTHOR

Photo by Nancy Heizer.

A central Kentucky native, Roy Heizer grew up visiting Cincinnati frequently. After spending several years in the Southeast, Roy and his wife, Nancy, settled in Cincinnati. He is the author of seven books: four on gardening, two books of ghost stories (*Haunted Charlotte* and *Cincinnati Cemeteries*) and one about the historic churches and synagogues of Savannah. The Heizers have traveled extensively around the world to research and photograph for writing projects. Nancy took the photographs for all their books. Roy has lectured and presented seminars on topics ranging from the history of religious rituals to the science and mythology of garden plants. He is a certified plant professional in three states. In addition to being an avid reader, writer and lecturer, Roy is a huge fan of classic horror and mystery films. He also admins a Facebook group, "Sinister Cincinnati."

The Heizers have two dogs and three cats.